A Challenged Life

A Challenged Life

raising a child with special needs

DANIELLE ZIMMERMAN

B.E.S.M. Inc.
Coral Springs, Florida

Published by
B.E.S.M. Inc.
Coral Springs, Florida
www.abisplace.com

Publisher's Cataloguing-in-Publication Data
Zimmerman, Danielle

    A challenged life : raising a child with special needs
/ Danielle Zimmerman. – Coral Springs, Fla. : B.E.S.M. Inc., 2010.

    p. ; cm.

    ISBN13: 978-0-9843896-0-5

    1. Children with mental disabilities—care. 2. Parent and child.
    3. Children with mental disabilities—Biography.
    4. Zimmerman family. I. Title.

HQ773.7.Z56 2010
649.1528—dc22   2010901301

Project coordination by Jenkins Group, Inc.
www.BookPublishing.com

Cover photograph by Monica Dyer, monicadyerphotography.com
Cover and interior design by Yvonne Fetig Roehler

FIRST EDITION

Printed in the United States of America
06 07 08 09 10 • 5 4 3 2 1

To Abigail

Contents

Introduction

I welcome you into my world in this book, to share my journey to help give parents comfort, revelation, and hope. Professionals in the health field and special education systems are also encouraged to read my story to help gain knowledge on issues that all parents go through when raising a child with special needs. I hope you find my story interesting, entertaining, and inspiring. If I can do it, so can you!

I see myself today as a child and parent advocate put on this earth, living this life that was chosen for me, to help children and families out there living on the roller coaster that accompanies raising a child with special needs. I want to share my journey to help others and inspire others to share their journeys with me.

Throughout the years, many people have asked me how I keep that smile on my face, even our therapists. Naturally, I am a glass half full kind of gal, and perhaps that is how I do it. However, the reality is that I have had my moments when I have cried, sobbed, screamed, gotten stupid drunk… I am human. We all have good days and not so good days but that is okay. There are always two ways to look at a situation, either as a problem or a blessing. I have chosen to look at my life as a blessing.

Yesterday a mom called me with questions on what she should be doing to help her child who isn't considered "typical" and who has a diagnosis of global delays. I found myself repeating the same words over and over: "Don't lose yourself." Remember, you are your daughter's mother but you are still an amazing woman and wife, too. She asked, "How did you keep your marriage together?" As you will learn further into the book, by not losing myself as the mother of a sick child. In other words, I had to keep the fun and sexy part of my life with my husband. The caller then asked, "How did you find out about Abigail's diagnosis?"

As you will see, it was a long process, and sometimes more answers were created than answered. Therefore, my wisdom nudged me to tell my new friend the deep truth I knew instinctively and that was confirmed over and over as our lives with Abi evolved: love is really all that matters. A diagnosis helps with services and insurance payments, but nothing will change the way you love your child.

1

A Daughter
Is Born

*T*he first two years of Abigail's life were hell. We didn't plan them to be. Of course, like all expectant parents, we were thrilled when we found out we were pregnant. We hadn't expected it to happen so quickly. For many years before we'd conceived, I'd had problems: several abnormal Pap smears and procedures to get rid of abnormal cells, irregular periods, a miscarriage and DNC, and finally severe pain that sent me to the hospital three different times. I'd also had two surgeries to remove scar tissue around my ovaries, so when my husband Brett and I decided we wanted to have a baby, we weren't sure if it would – or even could – happen.

I scheduled an infertility consultation to discuss my options with my ob/gyn, and he drew blood to test various hormone levels. When the results came back, he said we'd discuss our next step.

A week later, the nurse called me to tell me I would not be a candidate for infertility drugs or procedures because I was already pregnant!

Overjoyed, I ran out and bought a black and white card with a baby face on the front and a little pink baby dress. I just knew we were having a girl. I put the card in the dress and hung it in Brett's closet.

When he came home from work, he opened the closet to get changed and walked right back out, dumbfounded. "Uh, what does this mean?" he asked, completely perplexed.

"What do you think it means?" I said excitedly. "We're going to have a baby!"

Brett ran over and hugged me and we cried together.

Our initial high soon turned to apprehension. Brett has a genetic bone disorder called Osteogenesis Imperfecta (OI). People with the disorder are born without the ability to make collagen, so they have weak and brittle bones. All the men in Brett's family have this condition, and he was always led to believe it was a male-only disorder. By age 30, Brett had broken each leg eleven times, had crushed his knees, and had only partial kneecaps left. He was terrified he might have a boy with the same disease, so we prayed this baby was a girl.

I talked to my doctor about finding out the baby's gender as early as possible and asked for an amniocentesis. He laughed. "You're only twenty-three," he said. "There's no reason for an amnio." He did, however, promise that he was getting a three-dimensional-imaging ultrasound machine, the latest technology, and he'd give me one for free when it came in.

The machine never arrived, but my doctor reassured me he would do the regular ultrasound as early as possible. After all I'd been through with him over the past few years, I trusted my doctor and didn't think to question him.

When, at the first ultrasound, he told us the baby was a girl, Brett and I were thrilled. Our anxiety about having a baby with OI vanished; everything was going our way and the timing couldn't have been better. We'd been married three years and I was in my last year of undergraduate school. I would be pregnant while finishing school and studying for the Medical College Admission Test (MCAT), I'd apply to medical schools, and I'd deliver after final exams.

But you know what they say about the best-laid plans. At a routine ultrasound during my eighth month, two weeks before my final exams, the doctor told me our baby wasn't growing properly and he sent me to the hospital to deliver immediately.

Not surprising for me (you'll learn this about me as you read further), I remained calm. On the way to the hospital, I even ducked into Boston Market for a quarter chicken dark with mashed potatoes, creamed spinach, and of course, cornbread. (Any woman who's ever been pregnant can relate to how important food is.) Brett met me at the hospital and Abigail was born twenty-five hours later.

It was love at first sight. She was small, just shy of six pounds, with very skinny arms and legs. They looked like four bones with skin on them. At nineteen inches long, she fit perfectly into the crook of my forearm. Nobody seemed concerned about her size and the doctors told us she was completely healthy. Being a first-time mom, I was thrilled that she was petite. Thank goodness I didn't have to push a big baby out of my va jay jay! My parents said she looked like a porcelain doll and we agreed. She had no hair and her eyes were almond shaped and blue. She was flawless.

We took her home and everything was perfect for our new little family for seven whole days. Brett was an amazing father, taking Abigail through the whole house to show her every room with very detailed descriptions like "This is the kitchen where Mommy and Daddy cook for our family and friends." I remember enjoying every moment of breastfeeding and bathing our beautiful porcelain doll and I wore a smile of pure bliss from ear to ear. I never wanted to put her down, she fit so perfectly in my arms.

Then the nightmare began. In the middle of the night on her seventh night of life, Abigail began fussing, so I scooped her out of the bassinet that sat next to our bed. I propped myself up against the headboard and began to nurse her in the pitch-black bedroom. After only a few seconds, she fell off my breast and I felt her start almost pulsing. Her hands, arms, and legs seemed to be moving in a rhythmic pattern. I was startled, but the movement stopped pretty quickly and she fell back to sleep, so after looking her over and deciding that she seemed fine, just sleepy, I put her back into the bassinet and went back to bed.

I know, you're probably thinking I'm nuts. But remember, I had been pre-med for the past four years in college and I'd been studying for the MCATs so I knew there was nothing you could do for a seizure. It was four in the morning, the seizure had stopped, and she was sleeping calmly, so I decided it was best to wait until morning to call the pediatrician.

In the morning, over the telephone, the doctor disagreed with my seizure diagnosis. This was a startle reflex, he said, perfectly normal for infants Abi's age, and I had no reason to be concerned. I trusted his expertise and figured I must have been wrong. It hadn't been a seizure, just a normal startle reflex.

But after I hung up the phone I couldn't stop thinking about what had happened the night before. I turned it around in my mind a bit and tried not to worry, but I couldn't help it. Even though my mommy brain was only eight days old, it still worked well enough to tell me this hadn't been a normal startle reflex.

The next twenty-four hours went smoothly, but the night after that, Abigail had another seizure as I was feeding her that the doctor again retroactively called a startle reflex. She had another one the next night. A few days later, while nursing Abigail at my sister's house, it happened again.

Nicole went ballistic. "That is not normal!" she shouted, and insisted on taking us straight to the doctor.

We marched into the doctor's office, my brain screaming, "This is not a normal startle reflex!" I demanded the doctor test Abi to figure out what was causing the seizures. It took some convincing, but he finally agreed to do a spinal tap to rule out infections such as meningitis and encephalitis. A spinal tap is an incredibly intrusive procedure, but I knew she was having seizures and we had to find out why.

He drew the fluid, and miraculously, Abigail didn't even cry. All I kept thinking was, "What a good baby I have." Little did I know what was to come.

We needed to go to the emergency room to get the fluid tested, so we set off with our ten-day old baby and our bottle of spinal fluid. Remember how calm I was when the OB told me I needed to deliver immediately? I was the same way on our way to the ER. Calm, cool, and collected. I was in survival mode, and no emotions were necessary.

They admitted us to the general population floor for observation, but it was obvious that everyone thought we were overreacting. The nurse was pretty blasé when she evaluated Abi, but that soon changed when Abi had a seizure on the spot. I'm not sure the nurse had ever before seen an actual seizure – she literally stopped in her tracks and her eyes practically popped out of her head. She told us to grab our stuff because they were moving us to the Neonatal Intensive Care Unit (NICU), where they'd put Abi on much closer monitoring.

The emergency room visit turned into a two-week ordeal, and it was during this time we discovered our perfect little girl was far from perfect. The neurologists evaluating Abigail got our records from the OB floor and made a copy for us to look at. We soon made some disturbing discoveries. Abi was not, as my OB had indicated when she was born, a bouncing baby girl. She'd been diagnosed as having intrauterine growth retardation (IUGR), which meant she hadn't developed properly while in utero. And her APGAR, the test that assesses the health of a newborn immediately after birth, had been low. Even more disturbing was the reason why her scores were low. "Poor coloring, blue limbs," said the medical records.

Blue limbs? My stomach did a somersault when I read that. Why on earth had no one told me her limbs were blue at birth? Why had no one told me she had IUGR? Wasn't that something I needed to know?

I called my OB to ask why he hadn't told me about these problems. "I'm sitting in the hospital with a very sick little girl," I told him. "Why didn't you tell me this?"

His response was, "I told you she was small, but it wasn't my place to say anything more."

"You should have warned me!" I yelled into the phone. "We have a very sick baby and you didn't prepare me for this!"

There was silence at the other end of the line. Finally, after what seemed like forever, he replied, "I'm sorry you're going through this. If there's anything you need, let me know." Click…

Let him know? I did let him know! I'd needed a warning at Abi's birth, and now I needed an apology! I got even angrier and yelled into thin air, "You insensitive jerk!" I knew why he hadn't apologized. He was covering his own ass, and that only added to my fury.

I hung up in disbelief and disgust. If it wasn't his place to tell us our baby was sick, whose was it? All I could think was, "Why did I trust you in the first place?"

Meanwhile, our two-week-old baby lay in an incubator, unable to regulate her body temperature. I cried a lot, but only when I was alone. When friends and family came to visit I put on my happy face, which was much easier than letting them see my real feelings. I couldn't bear the thought of their pity. Inside, I was furious at the doctor for not telling me anything when she was born. If he knew she was small and had blue limbs and IUGR, why didn't he tell me? Why hadn't she stayed in the hospital longer?

But there wasn't time to dwell on these questions. We had to figure out why Abigail was having the seizures, and all the tests – from viral and bacterial meningitis to metabolic disorder to type 1 diabetes – came back negative. Our baby was sick, but we didn't know why.

Finally, when they ran out of tests to perform, they sent us home. We had no diagnosis, but they did give us a prescription for Phenobarbital, an anti-seizure medicine. We gave her the medicine as directed, and while they controlled the seizures somewhat, they made Abigail sleep all the time. In addition, she still had what they called break-though seizures – as she grew, the medication was no longer enough to control them. The treatment for that was more Phenobarbital, which tranquilized her even more.

Meanwhile, since I'd delivered early, I had been unable to take my final exams. My professors were all very sympathetic and let me take my finals after Abi came home after the seizure fiasco. Ironically, I passed with flying colors. It was one of my best semesters, but I still had one more semester before graduation. I'd planned to study for the MCATS throughout this semester, but those books were destined to sit on my shelf while my medical school applications collected dust on my desk. I occasionally looked at them with watery eyes and hoped that one day my dreams would come true. I had been working toward a career in medicine since I was in the ninth grade, collecting dissections like trophies. My prize possession was the cat brain that had taken me four days to get out.

I had been obsessed with becoming a doctor, but now I was consumed with something else – my precious baby. As the months went by, I enjoyed Abi's little awake periods for play and photo ops, but these positive times seemed to be decreasing. Week by week, everything got harder.

Feeding became a particular problem. I had immediately fallen in love with breastfeeding. That time together, looking down at my little baby's face, was a total love fest, but soon after Abi was born her suck began to weaken, so I started pumping my breast milk and feeding it to her out of the bottle. I wanted to breastfeed exclusively, but as she became weaker, she simply wasn't getting enough nourishment, so I made the tough decision to supplement her with formula.

Soon, even the formula wasn't helping. For every ounce she drank, she threw up half. Think Linda Blair in *The Exorcist* and you'll get an idea of what I was going through.

Nighttime was particularly challenging because Abigail cried nonstop. Her stomach bothered her so much that she simply couldn't get comfortable. She'd grimace, thrash about, and scream all night long. My husband was working two jobs at the time, but he didn't shirk his fatherly duties, taking the first shift until 2:00 a.m. Then he'd wake me up and I'd take over until the sun came up at 7:00 a.m. The only position Abi seemed to not hate was upright in the vibrating bouncy chair, so we'd put her in it and stand guard next to her the entire night.

Every two to three weeks we had to take Abi to the emergency room. She threw up so often that she became dehydrated, limp, pale, sleepy, and just plain lifeless. I almost think dehydration was worse than the seizures. It happened so often that the emergency personnel knew us on a first-name basis.

At one of our many visits, the on-call gastroenterologist asked us to follow up with him once we were home. We were optimistic that he could help the stomach problems. At first he diagnosed her with colic and showed us different ways to wrap her. He also suggested we keep her upper body elevated after she'd eaten so she could digest properly, but neither suggestion helped. Then he recommended over-the-counter Mylecon to help reduce the gas. I swear I went through an entire bottle every couple of days, but it did absolutely nothing. Then he gave me a prescription for Pepcid to combat the acid reflux. That too did nothing. We tried every different formula known to man, including the "extensively hydrolyzed formula," a.k.a., the type you have to take out a second mortgage on your house to afford because the proteins have already been predigested. But, unfortunately, the vomit kept coming.

Then we hit on the mother lode. The gastroenterologist diagnosed Abi with delayed gastric emptying, which meant the milk was literally sitting in her stomach so long that it was curdling. He prescribed a drug called Cisapride, which was supposed to help both the acid reflux and the delayed gastric emptying. And it did. I called it my miracle drug. I could literally hear the angels sing as Abi started throwing up, and crying, less.

But as luck would have it, the drug was pulled off the market only a few months after Abi started taking it. I swear, it worked so well I felt like crossing the border into Mexico to buy it. We switched to another drug and things went south again. Two months went by and Abigail was now taking three new medications, but she was still having problems. She was only getting the bare minimum for hydration so any time anything went wrong – say her sinuses backed up or her throat became sore – she'd get dehydrated within a matter of hours.

When Abigail got a cold, it was agonizing. She was unable to swallow properly and clear her mucus and everything would come up. By "up" I mean the drapes, the blankets, me, everything in sight would be covered with milk and mucus. My entire house smelled like a bottle of milk that had been left out in the Florida sun for three days. "Not pleasant" is an understatement.

Then, when Abigail was five months old, she completely shut down. I tried desperately to get her to nurse, but she wouldn't. My husband sat with her for hours, gently squeezing the milk drop by drop out of the bottle and into her mouth, but it just rolled down her cheeks. She would not suck at all, she was completely dehydrated, and after two weeks of this torture we took her back to the hospital. They told us they'd have to put in an IV to rehydrate her, but because she'd had so many IVs over the past few months, her veins were full of scar tissue. The only suitable veins they could find were the ones in her head.

We literally pleaded with Abi to eat. Not that she could understand of course, but we were desperate. Until she started to eat on her own, we were stuck in the hospital. The problem was, she was getting hydration but not nutrition from the IV in her head, so the doctor sat us down and explained the situation. He told us we had two weeks to get her to eat, and if we failed they'd start her on total parenteral nutrition (TPN), which meant she'd get all her nutrition through a feeding tube. Which did we prefer, that the feeding tube go in her nose, her stomach, or her intestines?

The conversation, which was deadly serious, was almost comical. I felt like I was in elementary school, sitting in a little chair in front of the doctor, with a hospital tray on wheels as a desk, as he began to draw me pictures. If the tube went in the nose, it would go down the esophagus and into the stomach, but that one could only be temporary. A more permanent solution was a feeding tube that went either directly into the stomach or, if she continued to throw up, into the intestines.

My head was spinning but I tried to stay as calm as possible. This decision could have life-long implications for our daughter. If it went in through her stomach she might still have the same digestive complications she had now – reflux and throwing up. If it went in the intestines, we'd bypass all that, but she'd never feel anything in her stomach. She'd never have that "I'm so hungry I could eat a horse" feeling or the "Oh, I'm so full I can't eat another bite" feeling.

Meanwhile, my husband was flipping out, saying "No" to everything. But something had to be decided and we were running out of time. The doctors told us that within two weeks, if she didn't get the feeding tube put in, she would have permanent brain damage.

We also had to decide whether or not to tie her stomach off to keep her from aspirating. Because she was vomiting so much, we were in constant fear the fluid from her stomach would go into her lungs. Tying off her stomach would keep her from aspirating, but it would also mean she'd never throw up again. Ever.

Remember those nights in college when you drank way too much and sat by the toilet, praying you'd throw up? All I kept thinking was that my baby would never be able to throw up again if we did the surgery, and I didn't know how to make this life-altering decision for her.

My husband and I were horribly frustrated, to say the least. It was a really emotional time. I'd been pumping breast milk this entire time, but Abi hadn't been nursing for a while now, so I was pumping and storing the milk in the freezer in the parents' lounge at the hospital. I had a ton of bottles, all with Abi's name on them, but they were never used. When I asked the doctor what would go in the feeding tube, he told me that I wasn't making enough breast milk to put in the tube, and at this point it wouldn't make much of a difference to Abigail anyway. After all the pumping I'd done, that just about killed me.

While all this was happening, I still didn't know the answer to the most important question: what was wrong with our baby? I felt like I was going through the five stages of grief – denial and isolation, anger, bargaining, depression, and acceptance – all in a matter of weeks. In retrospect, I think I probably was.

Finally, we decided to put the feeding tube through her nose. We'd decide something more long-term later, if she needed it. We also transferred Abigail to a new facility in Miami. We felt like the small hospital we'd been in had been putting Band-Aid after Band-Aid on her problem whereas we needed to get to the source of it.

Once we arrived in Miami, we immediately started meeting with doctors, nurses, students, and specialists – neurologists, geneticists, gastroenterologists, and infectious disease doctors. They drew blood to do genetic testing, they did a swallow test to see what was going on in the upper GI tract, they did a lower GI study, and they did more EEGs, a seizure workup, and another MRI. They were all willing to help with the current problems Abigail had and to search for the reason why they were happening.

To be honest, I wish I could give you every detail of that next two and a half weeks, but much of it is a blur. We began the hospital stay at West Boca Medical Center, then were transferred to Miami Children's for an additional two weeks. All told, Abi was in the hospital a little over two months in order to find out what was wrong and how to get her eating again.

When your baby is in the hospital for that long, your entire world changes. You get up in the morning and literally make a to-do list in your head: take a shower, make sure Abi gets a bath, make sure Abi gets her meds. Which doctor am I going to see today? Make a list of questions for that doctor.

I remember a lot of students going in and out of Abigail's room – this was a teaching hospital so they had to present her case every day. Other than that, most of it is a blur. What I remember most is that my husband and I were determined not to leave Miami Children's Hospital without answers.

2

Searching for
Answers

There we sat, trying to make it through each day at Miami Children's Hospital. We spent two weeks running tests and getting used to the new feeding tube that went in through Abi's nose, down through her esophagus, and into her stomach. She looked like an alien, with tape everywhere on her face holding the tube in place.

Abi was now eight months old, and boy, did she hate that tube. When it first went in she gagged constantly, but thank goodness that feeling subsided fairly quickly. But even after the retching stopped, she was constantly tugging at the tube with her little hands and shaking her head from side to side, trying to get it out of her nose. Sometimes, unfortunately, she succeeded. The nurses taught us how to get it back in since we'd eventually have to do it ourselves, but it was torture. It took two or three people to hold her down while she gagged, screamed, and cried.

I was desperate to save my little girl from the agony of the tube reinsertion, so I tried to get creative in taping it down so she couldn't pull it out. I was pretty handy with a piece of tape, since I'd volunteered in an emergency room during college and had some EMT training under my belt. I was able to use both hands to their full capacity – I cut the strips of tape with one hand and painted her little face with the adhesive liquid with the other. Then I'd tape the feeding tube onto her face, leading it out her nostril, up to her cheekbone, and around her ear.

I knew that visitors – even our closest family – would gawk and stare no matter how the tape looked, but still I couldn't help trying to make it look pretty. And heck, Abi was a beautiful little girl if I do say so myself. I didn't want that entire adorable face completely covered by adhesive tape and tubing.

The feeding team and gastroenterologist kept throwing around the words "failure to thrive," a medical term I tried not to let scare me. The term made it seem like Abigail was on hospice, ready to die any minute. But of course, that wasn't the case at all. So instead of letting the medical term paralyze me, I put a sensible perspective on it. In my head, I broke down the words. "Failure" equals unable, and "to thrive" means to live on her own.

"Well, sure she couldn't live on her own. She's a baby for goodness sake," was my conclusion. I took what they said and didn't let it phase me. I went through the motions and didn't think about the future while the doctors continued to do test after test, including a genetic test my husband and I both gave blood for.

At some point we met with yet another neurologist. After he evaluated Abigail and assessed her abilities, he told us she was developmentally delayed. She wasn't doing anything an eight-month-old baby should be doing. She wasn't rolling, exploring her body, babbling, bearing weight on her feet, sitting up, holding up her head, and the list went on. Not only was she not doing what a typical eight-month-old baby was doing, she wasn't even doing what a typical three-month-old baby should be doing. (See the Resource Guide at the back of the book for information on the developmental milestones for babies.)

This wasn't news to us. I had brought these concerns to Abi's new pediatrician at her four-month check-up back in August. She'd told me to wait and see. But now, the hospital neurologist gave me his developmentally delayed diagnosis and ordered a battery of tests.

Through all this torture, the one milestone Abi didn't miss was smiling. Boy, could that little girl smile. At five weeks, her smile had lit up the room, and even through the horrible crying-filled nights, Abi's days were filled with smiles. They kept me going.

Her grin went from ear to ear – all gums, of course. Everyone commented on her smile. It was contagious, and once you saw her smile, you couldn't help but smile back, sometimes even laugh. Her smile could turn a bad day into a good day just like that, and all the pain and suffering went away, if only momentarily, in that moment of pure, innocent happiness. I am sure any mom or dad can relate.

After two weeks at Miami Children's Hospital, just like at the last hospital, they ran out of tests to do. Abi was doing well with her feeding tube and had gained appropriate weight, so they sent us home. We had no diagnosis, but the results of many of the tests still weren't in. Maybe the answer was hidden in one of them?

A few weeks later the day arrived for our follow-up with the geneticist. My husband and I packed up Abigail along with the diapers, wipes, and a change or two of clothing for her and drove the hour-plus to Miami.

Frankly, I didn't think the geneticist was going to give us any answers. I was just going through the motions, meeting with everyone I was supposed to, running the suggested tests, and never really getting any resolution. But from the start, I had liked the geneticist. She had always spoken gently and seemed very sincere. She'd also set us straight on Brett's OI. When we'd first met, while going over family history, we'd told her that Brett had OI, which was why we'd been so thrilled to be having a girl.

She'd looked confused, and after Brett said that he, his father, and grandfather all had OI, she'd interrupted and said "OI is not an X or Y gene." Then the confused look moved to Brett's face and he told the doctor his grandfather had told him only boys could get OI.

She'd shaken her head and said that wasn't true. Because Brett had the gene and I did not, there was a fifty percent chance, every time we got pregnant, that our child would have OI, regardless of whether that child was a boy or a girl.

At that point, we felt lucky that Abi didn't have OI. Here we'd thought we'd dodged a bullet because she was a girl when in fact she could have had OI on top of all her other problems!

For the follow-up visit with the geneticist, Brett and I walked into the office with Abi in the stroller. We each sat down on a chair, with the doctor on her rolling stool. She opened the file from the lab and reviewed a simple genetic mapping, a layout of chromosomes, and gave us a copy. The picture looked like a bunch of little bricks with X's, and though I'd studied basic genetic mapping in college, nothing on the page jumped out at me as wrong.

But there was something wrong. The doctor told us that Abigail had a mutation in her chromosomes that neither Brett nor I had. Genetic information, she explained, is stored in twenty-three pairs of chromosomes. Chromosomes are made of DNA, and genes are special units of chromosomal DNA. DNA can be likened to a set of blueprints that basically contain all the instructions needed to construct the body of a human being.

Abi, she explained, had something called a translocation. This meant that portions of two chromosomes – in Abi's case, numbers nine and thirteen – had switched places. Translocations can be balanced, in which there's an even exchange of material and no genetic information is missing, or they can be unbalanced, in which the exchange of chromosome material is unequal, resulting in either extra or missing genes. A lot of people actually have balanced translocations. You may have one and have no idea, because when no genetic material is lost, the person is perfectly normal.

But Abi was not normal, and the geneticist theorized her trans-location was unbalanced. If indeed this was the case, she would be the first person in the world known to have this exact mutation. At the same time, because there was no medical literature on this exact mutation, the doctor wasn't positive if this was the cause of her problems. The doctor's tone and demeanor were very blasé, so mine stayed blasé as well.

The geneticist told us she wanted to test Abi for another genetic abnormality called Angelman Syndrome. One of the main symptoms, she told us, was a very happy baby. Since Abigail was full of smiles for the majority of the daytime, she thought it was worth a shot.

I walked out of the office feeling somewhat better – it looked like we had a missing piece of the puzzle, and even though a big chunk of information was still missing, we were going to search until we found it.

Before we'd even seen the geneticist, we'd decided to get a second opinion from another gastroenterologist and a neurologist. My in-laws and my husband were New Yorkers who only believe in New York medicine, but we'd all agreed the University of Miami, Jackson Hospital, would have great doctors, so we'd made an appointment with their gastroenterologist and neurologist weeks before we saw the geneticist.

On the day of this appointment, several weeks after our second appointment with the geneticist, we drove an hour and forty-five minutes to get there, then waited an hour for the first doctor to tell us what we already knew: Abi was failing to thrive, though she was surviving on the feeding tube and pre-digested formula. We learned we would still have to make a more permanent decision about putting the feeding tube in the stomach or the intestines. And, in this doctor's opinion, we should tie her stomach to keep her from throwing up. No new news, and no good news.

After we were done, we waited another two hours to meet with the neurologist. When we finally got into the room, my husband and I sat down in two plastic chairs with Abi in my lap. The doctor stood up across from us, his arms crossed. He had a very straight, unemotional look on his face. Perhaps Abi was his last patient of the day and he was just exhausted, but his demeanor did not bode well for our meeting. He took an entire five minutes to examine Abigail, checking her reflexes and measuring her head circumference. Then Dr. Bedside Manner said, "She is microcephalic."

My husband and I looked at each other like, "What is that?" None of the hundreds of doctors we'd seen had ever mentioned that term. The next words that came out of his mouth are to this day seared into my brain. Even writing this, the tears still well up in my eyes. He explained unemotionally, "That means she will be like a monkey, with no reasoning or logical thinking."

"What?" Brett yelled.

"That is the difference between humans and monkeys," Dr. Bedside Manner said. "Humans have logical thinking. Your daughter does not."

I remained composed, though it felt like a dagger had just punctured my heart. I thought Brett was going to haul off and sock the doctor, but amazingly, he refrained. Brett had never punched anyone in his life, but his eyes were fiercer than I'd ever seen them in the entire time I'd known him.

I gave Abi a squeeze, stood up with her in my arms, and walked toward the door. Brett followed my lead. I was actually polite, telling Dr. Bedside Manner, "Goodbye, and thank you for your time." I walked out of the office and down the hospital corridor.

That car ride home was very quiet. I remember weeping, and I actually made Brett pull over to buy a pack of cigarettes so I could smoke my first cigarette in eighteen months. My husband walked around the next few days like a zombie, in complete disbelief. While Abigail was sleeping throughout the days, I googled the internet for everything I could find about microcephaly. The more I researched, the more depressed I became.

The term, which I should have known since I'd taken medical terminology in college, simply means "small brain or head" ("micro" means small, "cephaly" means brain or head). Indeed, Abi's head circumference was well below the norm on the charts, and when I looked back on her birth record, it measured below the norm I found on the internet.

My research laid out the problems that accompany this diagnosis. Number one, seizures. Other symptoms include mental retardation, difficulty with body movements and speech, and typically a short life span. Microcephaly is clinically linked to infants with growth problems and/or genetic abnormalities. The diagnosis flashed like a bright yellow neon sign in a dark alley. Blink blink blink. This was it. It made sense, and it explained everything.

I searched back through the medical documents my ob/gyn had written on the day Abigail was born. The nurses and doctors had written the number of her head circumference as eleven inches. The average head circumference of a newborn is fourteen inches. Abigail was microcephalic at birth. And yet, no one ever wrote a diagnosis, though I am not sure why. No one called a neurology consult, and I am not sure why. Nine months later, we were finally putting the pieces together, but we could and should have had these answers the day she was born.

I felt so betrayed by my doctor. He and I had been so close. Before I'd become pregnant with Abi I'd had many problems, and he'd been there to walk me through all of them. We had hugged and kissed on the cheek every time we saw each other and spent hours talking about spouses, families, morals, values, and lifetime goals. How could he have just left me in the dark like this? And, if I'd had the amniocentesis like I'd wanted, I'd have known about all this before Abi was even born. I blamed him for failing me. Not just as my doctor, but as my friend.

Day after day I spent hours in front of the computer and talking to my mom on the phone while we did research together. I was in shock, and the tears kept coming. Why was this happening to Brett and me and to our daughter?

My mouth hit the floor when I read the description of a microcephalic baby. It sounded like most cases were a result of poor prenatal care. Could I have done this to Abi? No, there was no way. I had taken very good care of myself. I'd quit smoking, I'd carried healthy snacks with me, I'd drunk lots of water, I'd taken my prenatal vitamins, I'd eaten nutritious foods, and I'd gotten a lot of rest. What had gone wrong? Then I read the part about the genetic component and put the two together. Apparently our new geneticist had found the answer.

I started emailing a microcephalic support group I found on one of my many google searches. This was in some ways comforting but in many ways just more depressing. I spent hours chatting back and forth with other families. We all shared stories and doctor tales. We compared symptoms and I discovered that a lot of the other children had seizures, feeding problems, and weak muscles just like Abigail, and all of them were developmentally delayed. One girl was sixteen with the mental capacity of a six-month-old. I vicariously experienced "shout outs" over the internet to families that had just buried their microcephalic child.

Oh my god, death. Was Abigail going to die prematurely? What was her life expectancy? Would she progress beyond the mental capacity of a six-month-old? Would people be giving us shout outs in a few years? What did the future hold?

There were many more questions than answers. While I felt overwhelmed by the unknown, Brett was in denial and didn't want to know what I'd found on the computer. He slipped into depression pretty quickly, sleeping a lot and then eventually immersing himself in work. I tried to be supportive of other families online, but it was hard when I was just trying to deal with my own daughter. I didn't really feel like I had anything under control or organized. I was just existing one day at a time, barely getting out of my pajamas or showering. I felt an enormous amount of sadness. I didn't speak to anyone other than my mom and husband. We locked ourselves in the house, clothes and dishes piled everywhere.

Then one day I was standing in the kitchen, trying to put a dent in the disaster we'd let pile up around us for the past week. Brett was sleeping on the couch, Abigail was in her bouncy chair, and I was washing dishes with tears rolling down my face. I was so angry that

I felt helpless. This life was so different than the life I'd imagined. Abigail wouldn't do the things I'd done as a child like dancing, sports, and gymnastics, and this made me cry more.

Finally, it truly hit me and I let it all out. I allowed the medical terminology and the doctors get to me. All the grim diagnoses and the possibility that Abigail could die overwhelmed me. How long did I have with her? I didn't know.

After standing in my own misery for a while and thinking about my husband's misery, something else hit me as well. I was not behaving like the normal Danielle I knew. I was a "glass half full" kind of girl. Feeling this way was enough to make me sick and I knew I couldn't go on like this any longer. I knew I needed help, and the first step to turning everything around was to change my thinking.

I was looking at it all wrong. I wiped the tears away and went to my computer, where I deleted everything I had downloaded. I erased it from the hard drive of my memory as well as my desktop. None of it mattered. While it was true that my life and the life of our daughter was not going to be what we had expected, I still had hope. Hope that some day Abigail would be all that she could be.

I was willing to do everything in my power to help Abi achieve her full potential. Who said she couldn't dance, play sports, or do gymnastics? She might not be in the Olympics, but she could be in the Special Olympics. She might not be able to do the Hustle herself, but I'd put on a waltz, hold her in my arms, and dance her around the house. I was going to make the best life for Abigail I possibly could. And for our family. I was going to create a happy life, microcephaly be damned.

3

Therapy Begins

I was ready to help my little girl, but I had no idea how to start. Whom should I call? What should I do? Whom should I see? We visited our local neurologist, who gave us a prescription for therapy: occupational therapy four times a week, physical therapy four times a week, and speech therapy four times a week.

The neurologist recommended a place called the Davis Therapy Center, which was about forty-five minutes away from us. We live in South Florida, perhaps better known as retirement central. There are therapy centers on every corner, but this was the place the doctor recommended. Though it was quite a trek, I figured he knew best, so I called and made the appointments.

Abigail was ten months old when we started therapy, and I soon learned that just making it to the appointments on time felt like half the battle. Feeding utensils, toys, diapers, wipes, drinks, snacks, all the things she needed for therapy…

The diaper bag became my equivalent of a businessman's briefcase, filled with the essentials to get the job done. Therapy was four days a week, an hour and half each day, consisting of one half hour each of speech therapy, physical therapy, and occupational therapy.

This hour and a half commute and hour and a half in therapy four days a week was very time-consuming. In fact, it took up so much of my time that I literally made it my full-time job. Brett and I had started our own telemarketing company in 1996 with about fifty people. Brett ran the office while I took care of all the financials such as payroll, bills, employee benefits, unemployment claims, bookkeeping, taxes, and audits. But because I needed to focus solely on Abigail, we had to hire an assistant at the office to take over for me.

One day, as Abi's occupational therapist walked me down the hallway, she said, "It's too bad she can't handle longer sessions; I think we could make more progress." I could see the frustration on her face, and of course, I too wished Abi could handle more, but she just wasn't strong enough. The minute any of the therapists challenged her, she would resist and end up in tears. I couldn't get past my instinct to comfort her with my words, my emotions, and my body, and it took so much time reassuring Abi that she was okay and could do this that she missed a lot of good therapy time.

Nonetheless, all of the therapies were a learning experience, and I'd listen and watch every moment, diligently taking notes while Abi did her thing. I was an eager student willing to learn, the nerd in the first row who asks too many questions. Everything was new to me, but I had a natural love for medicine and for the human body, so everything I learned was fascinating.

I'm not sure if the therapists viewed me as annoying or just extremely interested, but I didn't care. I was doing what was best for my daughter. I asked what exercise ball I should buy to use with Abigail? What toys should I buy to help her move and use her hands better? What high chair should I buy to help with feedings as she progressed? The therapists were my professors, my support system, my mentors.

Speech therapy, I learned, was not actually teaching Abigail to talk. She was, after all, only ten months old, but this therapy would help give her the building blocks for eating and talking both.

When we started therapy, Abi hadn't eaten anything by mouth in four months. Not only had she not wanted to eat because of all the vomiting, she'd also lost the ability to suck and swallow due to a brain injury.

Yes, you read that right. Shortly after therapy started, we learned that Abigail had a brain injury. She'd been getting regular MRIs, and the neurologist had phoned to tell us that between two of them – the one he'd done when she was six months old and the one he'd done right before we started therapy when she was nine months old, Abigail's brain had shrunk. He didn't know why – perhaps it was due to the seizures, or perhaps due to the genetic abnormality itself – but it explained why she had so much trouble eating when we were in the hospital during that last visit.

So now, not only were we dealing with Abigail not wanting to eat, her brain showed that she physically didn't know how to eat. Almost like a stroke patient, she'd have to learn how to eat all over again.

For most children, coordinating the tongue, gums or teeth, and cheeks so that they can eat and talk comes naturally. But not for Abigail; we would have to teach her how to do every one of these things.

In my head I was sad, but on the outside I stayed positive. We just had to work harder. I knew there was nothing we could do about what had happened, but we could help Abi create new pathways in the brain to help make up for the deficits.

But before we could do anything, we had to get Abigail to stop resisting anything near her face. When any of us got anywhere near her mouth, she'd pull back and tighten her lips like they were sealed with superglue. Occasionally she would cry, but she avoided crying at all costs because that meant opening her mouth a bit, which gave us a chance to get in there.

We had to gain her trust, and that meant working from the outside in. We started with a soft washcloth to massage the outside of the face, which stretched the muscles and helped Abigail get more comfortable with having her face touched. She was petrified when someone came at her face and recoiled again and again, but the more we did it, the more comfortable she became. I can't say she ever learned to enjoy it, but she did eventually back up less.

During physical and occupational therapy I brought note pads and wrote down exercises to do at home. I spent each session watching intently, studying exactly where the therapist put her hands and how she maneuvered Abigail's hands, legs, and torso. I wanted to make sure I was doing it just like the therapist. There were even times when the therapists coached me and I ran the session.

Some exercises were as simple as having Abi bear weight on her hands. Abigail would lie on her tummy and push and hold herself up. Sounds simple, yes, but Abigail didn't like, no, she *hated* to be on her tummy. It put pressure on her stomach, which pushed the acid up her esophagus. But I knew she had to push anyway, because this exercise was key to strengthening her back, shoulders, and hands, which was crucial for her development.

At ten months, Abi still wasn't sitting up or even rolling over, and getting her to rotate her trunk from right to left – something she needed to do to reach those milestones – was not easy either. She was a virtual sack of potatoes. She had developed scoliosis, a curvature of the spine, from the low muscle tone and her delayed development, and she had no coordination or balance.

To help stretch her back and shoulders, we placed Abi on the ball. The therapist had one hand on a leg and the other hand on Abi's opposite arm and she gently stretched her. Other times we worked on her trunk rotation on a mat to help her learn to roll over. We also used the ball to work on sitting up. Fortunately, like most children, Abi loved the ball.

One of us would stand in front of Abi, holding her legs steady on the floor, while the other placed her hands on Abi's back. Slowly, the person supporting her back would ease up so that Abigail could learn to rely on her own muscles to balance on the ball.

Baby sit-ups were another favorite of the therapists, though not of Abi's. We lay her on the floor and held her hands and pulled her up lightly, letting her do some of the work. Eventually, we hoped, she would get so good at sit-ups that we wouldn't have to help at all.

Watching Abigail work showed me how much I took moving my body for granted. Crawling, the physical therapist explained, uses all the major muscles in our bodies. In order to get Abigail to use those muscles, we had to strengthen them individually, then pattern Abigail's brain to coordinate these muscles by physically doing the activity for her.

"Patterning the brain" sounds fancier than it is. It means that the more you do something, the more likely your brain will remember it. When something is repeated enough times in your short-term memory, it is transferred into your long-term memory. For example, if you dial a phone number over and over, you're likely to remember it.

In Abi's case, we tried to pattern her brain to perform a protective reaction – putting her hands down to stop herself from falling, for example. Most babies are born with this instinct, but not Abi. She had to learn it. So we gently pushed Abigail to the side, then physically put her hands down for her. We'd do it over and over again, and eventually she did it on her own.

As time went on, I realized I was learning the tricks of the trade. I was Abigail's therapist at home during the fifty-two hours each week she was awake but not in formal therapy. This was very important, because the six hours a week she spent with the therapists weren't enough to make significant progress. It was therefore my job to follow through with these exercises at home.

To that end, we spent every afternoon working on exercises like holding toys in her hands, helping her move a toy from one hand to the other, and reaching for toys to the sides of her. I bought a peanut ball (a plastic ball shaped like, you guessed it, a peanut) and I lay her on top of it on her belly and tilted the ball forward so she'd be forced to bear weight on her hands. I also made her do baby sit-ups holding my hands while lying on the floor, and I moved her legs like a motor boat, kicking them back and forth.

I probably had an advantage, being a physically fit person myself and knowing the muscles in the body, but it was as simple as doing an exercise video, and I tried to make it fun for both of us.

After six months of therapy, Abi was making progress, albeit very slowly. She could hold one toy but not two. She was learning to balance herself in a sitting position but was still falling to the sides when she reached away from her body. She was holding her head up but not straight. This was because she had torticollis, a condition in which the neck muscles are extremely tight on one side, which pulls the head in a cockeyed direction. The therapist told me the only way to help it was to stretch her neck, so during therapy we always spent ten minutes pulling and stretching while Abigail screamed and screamed. I also tried to stretch her at home, though I must admit I never did it with the therapist's intensity. When I did it, it was more like moving her head to the opposite side for a minute or so.

Abi also refused to bear weight on her hands and knees in the crawling position. The only way to get her to do this was to do it for her, using my two hands on her legs, the therapist's hands on her wrist, and a bolster underneath. Oh boy, Abigail did not like that.

When therapy began to feel like torture, we'd let Abi rest and get love. To be honest, I needed to pause and reassure her and myself that we were doing this for a good reason, but the more I let her get out of therapy by screaming and crying, the worse things got. She learned quickly how to manipulate to get those breaks and cuddle times, and by giving in to her time and again, I inadvertently reinforced bad behavior. Soon enough, very little of each session was actually spent doing therapy, with the bulk of each session spent trying to calm Abigail.

When I finally realized that coddling her was hindering her progress, we switched to tough love. We started using behavioral psychology and positive reinforcement to encourage her to make it through a thirty-minute session. For instance, we would do an activity like weight bearing and at the same time Abigail would get her favorite toy. Once she held that position for fifteen seconds we would give her a break but also take the toy away. In doing this again and again, she realized that doing something she didn't want to do would give her the reward she wanted. Eventually, she was thinking more about the reward rather than the fact that her muscles were working so hard.

I must admit, I asked so many questions that I was somewhat guilty of taking up therapy time myself. I wanted to learn how to do the therapies myself, so I questioned constantly and participated as much as I could. But it came in handy. I had been putting off a stomach surgery for Abi that would take away the acid reflux, not allow Abi to throw up ever again, and put a permanent feeding tube in her belly.

At the doctor's insistence, I finally took her in for the surgery, but what was supposed to be a three-day stay in the hospital turned into a three-month nightmare. Complications from the surgery left Abigail vomiting persistently for weeks. The surgery does keep children from throwing up, but if they try really hard over and over they will eventually bring something up, which was the case for Abigail. This retching occurred over and over again for months. We increased her medication and venting her tube so the pressure wouldn't build up in her belly and eventually the retching subsided, but we were out of our routine for a long time. The therapists couldn't come to the hospital, so I continued doing the exercises with her for the three months she was hospitalized, and that meant all my pestering paid off.

When she was eighteen months old, Abi sat up by herself. Brett and I couldn't contain our happiness when she finally hit this milestone. Nonetheless, after almost a year at the Davis Therapy Center, I decided we needed a change. I was exhausted by the drive and I thought Abigail could benefit from switching therapists. By 2001, we were enrolled in Medicaid's Early Intervention Program, a nationwide program to help children ages birth to three with birth problems and/or developmental delays. The Early Intervention Program provided therapy at home, and I was psyched. No more bags and no more driving. In addition,

Abigail could finally break that association of bad memories and torture therapy at the rehab center.

Early Intervention gave us a list of therapists in our neighborhood and I went down the list, calling them one by one to see who was available. I saw each initial meeting as a trial run. Because I'd already had a year of this, I was able to see the difference between a good and bad therapist and I realized I had to weed through the bad ones in order to get to the good.

Although it sounds counterintuitive, not all pediatric therapists know how to work with kids. They need to have enormous patience and be able to get down to a kid level, playing games, singing songs, and communicating with children on their own level.

Not all of them do. One physical therapist, for example, came and evaluated Abi. At the next appointment, she did the same exact thing. And the next time, and the next. She wasn't actually providing therapy to Abi, and I got rid of her.

Another disaster was the speech therapist who came into the room moving ninety-five miles an hour. She never made nice with Abigail, never spoke to her, never did anything but sit down and begin her exercises. Abigail immediately withdrew and resisted her. I tried to comfort Abi by telling her what was going on, singing songs, and trying to make it a positive experience. Then suddenly one day the therapist said to me, "I don't think Abigail is making any progress and I would like to discontinue our services."

No kidding? In hindsight, I should have discontinued the services weeks before the therapist did.

I learned from my mistakes with the next speech therapist. She walked in and sat Abi on her lap in front of the mirror right away. Forget introductions, forget getting comfortable, it was straight to business with this woman. She went right for Abi's mouth with her finger and Abi flipped out. That didn't stop this therapist. She put some food on a toothbrush and Abi went ballistic.

I snatched Abi out of her lap and asked her to try something different. We put her in the swing, and just as Abi was calming down the therapist came right back at her again with the food-soaked toothbrush.

Um, hello? I actually gave that therapist two more chances and then requested a switch.

The timing was perfect. A physical therapist we worked with recommended Rachel, who was so popular she had a long waiting list. Right when I let the all-business therapist go, something opened up in Rachel's schedule and I jumped at it.

Immediately, I saw why she had such a long wait list. Rachel became Abigail's friend. She got Abi to do things nobody else had even come close to. She played games like "Let me see your tongue" in which Abigail stuck out her tongue and Rachel said, "I'm gonna get it" while grabbing her tongue for a moment.

Abigail actually let her touch her tongue! I know it sounds a bit weird, but first off, nobody had been able to get near Abigail's mouth, let alone stick their hand in there and grab her tongue. And two, this was a great tongue strengthener, which would help develop the muscles so eventually Abi could speak.

Rachel also worked on strengthening Abi's jaw. She took gum in a gauze pad and held it between Abi's molars and had her bite down five to ten times. Over time, we worked up to rubbery toys designed specifically for oral motor strengthening. (See the Resource Guide at the back of the book for places you can find oral motor tools.)

Rachel also worked to stretch Abi's facial muscles, which were tight from lack of use (talking and eating naturally stretch your facial muscles). Rachel took a washcloth and gently applied pressure, starting from the high cheekbone and working her way diagonally toward Abi's mouth. She also used the cloth from the side of Abi's nose down to her lips.

Eventually, Rachel even got Abigail to eat candy. Okay, Abi didn't really bite or chew the candy, but she did put her tongue on and around a lollipop, which Rachel used as a tool for oral motor exercises. It was a two-for-one, in my eyes: Rachel got Abigail to really love her (by bribing her with candy!), and it was a wonderful oral motor exercise because the sugar made Abi produce more saliva, which she had to work hard to swallow.

Another of Rachel's techniques was to put flavored sugar on Abi's tongue. In response, Abi would move her tongue in and out of her mouth. I loved watching, and every once in awhile I'd catch a glimpse of myself in the mirror, with a smile and watery eyes. Once Rachel gained Abi's trust, everything was so much easier. Rachel was able to strengthen Abi's jaw, get her tongue to move in all directions, and loosen up her facial muscles.

After just a few months of working with Rachel, Abigail was actually trying real food! Some was successful, but since certain textures made Abi gag, Rachel suggested we do a swallow study, which uses an x-ray to see how food and drink move through the mouth and into the esophagus during chewing and swallowing.

This was a disgusting test, but it would tell us why Abi was choking all the time, so I knew we had to get through it. First, the radiologist took the food we brought – milk, baby food, and Cheerios – and mixed them with barium, a chalk-like liquid that lights up on the x-ray. (I couldn't help but wonder how accurate this test really was. I mean, who can really swallow chalk without hesitating?)

At any rate, we fed Abigail this barium mixture and the radiologist took continuous pictures to identify where the food was going. Up the nose? Down the sides of the throat? In the lungs? Or down the correct way in the center of the throat?

Abigail actually did pretty well with baby food – it went down her throat – but liquids and solids were another story. The doctors determined that she had oral dysphasia, which meant she had difficulty transferring food from her mouth to the back of the throat. People with oral dysphasia often don't chew their food fully and big pieces can get stuck, causing them to choke. When Abigail drank it was even worse, going all over the place, including up the nose and occasionally in the lungs.

Because she did okay with pureed baby food, we had something. Now we knew she could eat, the food just had to be the right consistency. We hoped over time her muscles would get stronger. Stronger muscles and better coordination meant she would be able to control all food consistencies and liquids.

After the swallow study, I spoke to my gastroenterologist about the results and we also discussed my frustration about Abi's progress in speech therapy. I felt like we were on the cusp. She was almost able to eat; we just needed to push her a little more. He mentioned a patient of his who had gone to an intensive feeding program in Baltimore, Maryland, and suggested we check it out.

I got right on the computer and gathered information about the Kennedy Krieger Institute, a comprehensive facility with one of the country's few intensive feeding programs. I thought it was worth a shot, so I called to set up an evaluation.

About three months later, in July of 2001, Abigail and I flew to Baltimore to see if she qualified for the twelve-week intensive feeding program. Because she had such an extensive history of problems, they insisted on performing two weeks' worth of testing before they evaluated her.

Since Kennedy Krieger is affiliated with Johns Hopkins, one of the best hospitals in the world, I decided to take advantage of all they had to offer. Accordingly, I set up consults with their neurologist, gastro-enterologist, and their behavior and rehabilitations team.

Every day, Abi had one or another test, including an upper GI series, which uses x-rays to show doctors what's going on during digestion in the stomach and small intestines; metabolic testing, which uses blood work to rule out any other genetic problem with food intake and the breakdown of food; a BMR calculator, which calculates how many calories you burn at rest; a mammotry test, which measures how the stomach and intestines contract to move food through the digestive system; a psychological evaluation; and an MRI. In other words, she had the works.

We learned that Abi's metabolic functions were normal but her digestion was slow because her stomach didn't contract properly to push food into the intestines. Her body was only burning 500 calories a day, which is low for someone her age. No wonder she was so roly poly – the doctors in Florida had told us to feed her 1,100 calories a day through the feeding tube. Thank god we found that out or my back might not have survived!

Unfortunately, another two weeks later the feeding team told us that Abigail was not ready for the intensive feeding program. Because their program was behavior-based, they wanted her to be eating at least an ounce of food orally in one seating. Though I was disappointed, I understood why they couldn't take her. And something equally as important came of the Kennedy Krieger visit: we decided to take advantage of the in-house intensive behavior program. I will go much more into this part of the program in the next chapter, but in a nutshell, we spent the next eight weeks in the Institute, with therapy lasting up to six hours a day.

Brett visited as much as he could, but since our stay was very expensive and insurance only paid for seventy percent of the treatment, he needed to stay in Florida and work. We made the best out of it, traveling on weekends around Maryland, Pennsylvania, and Washington DC. We made friends at the hospital and enjoyed hospital organized parties for the in-patients.

Toward the end of our stay in Baltimore, I had a revelation: Abigail needed every day to be like our days in Baltimore, with their six hours of intensive therapy. Could we do this? During one of Brett's visits, I told him that Abigail and I were going to come home different. We had learned so much from this trip medically and psychologically. I had studied with new physical, occupational, and speech therapists. In addition, the world of behavioral psychology had opened for me. I now understood why certain behaviors happened. I had learned to analyze them and how to redirect them. I also learned more about our daughter, including her feelings and frustrations.

My husband understood my new light and he motivated me to create our own Kennedy Kreiger Institute in our home in Coral Springs, Florida. As soon as we came home, we hired two physical therapists, two occupational therapists, and two speech therapists.

We included in our team several school teachers to help with school readiness skills. Some were provided to us through the public school system and some we paid privately. We did aqua therapy and hypo therapy (riding horses). We brought on a massage therapist to help with Abi's scoliosis, and we also started working with an acupressurist and cranial sacral therapist.

Some Things I Learned from My Experiences with the Therapists

1. Know the difference between good and bad therapists:
    - Is this a "kid" person?
    - Does this person talk with your child rather than at your child? (A therapist should ask questions, not make demands.)
    - Does this person challenge your child or are the same activities repeated over and over?
    - Do you have a good relationship with your therapist? (You should be able to say anything to this person. In turn, your therapist should be able to answer any questions, comments, or concerns without making you feel like you're asking too much.)
    - Does your therapist ask for your input or your thoughts and concerns?

2. If you're doing a home-therapy program:
    - Know what your goals are and what the therapist's goals are. (They should be the same.)
    - Ask what activities you can do at home to help reach these goals.
    - Participate in therapy or ask how you can help. (Not all parents can participate if the child will not work with you around, but still ask how you can help.)
    - Make time for home therapy just like you would for homework.
    - Make it fun!
    - See the Resource Guide at the back of the book for additional resources and other therapy ideas.

If you can't afford therapy, remember that every state has programs available for children ages birth to three. Contact your local department of children and family services to find out more details. In addition, if you are not enrolled with your state's Medicaid department, I highly recommend this resource. Some states offer more assistance than others, and every little bit helps.

4

Behavioral Issues

*B*elieve it or not, in spite of all the medical problems Abigail had and all the difficult medical decisions we had to make, her behaviors were what scared us the most. Let me go back in time a bit, when Abigail was about a year old and began to rock her head and body back and forth in the highchair. Oddly enough, when she hit the back of the chair, she didn't get scared. On the contrary, she seemed to enjoy it. Brett and I thought it was odd, but we weren't too concerned until her behavior progressed.

Soon, she was lifting her hand straight up and whacking herself in the head with her arm. She'd also try to hit herself harder and harder on the back of the highchair.

I tried not to worry. She wasn't able to talk, so perhaps this was her way of communicating, of trying to get my attention. I'd ask her, "Abi, do you need something?" but she'd continue to hit herself, giving me no indication of what she wanted, so I'd ask again and again, "Abi, what do you need?"

I knew she couldn't talk and that she wasn't going to burst out with a full sentence along the lines of, "Oh yes, Mom, I would like that toy Elmo over there staring at me." But I did hope for an eye glance or gesture that I could pick up to clue me in on what she wanted. Just like a baby crying out of hunger or to be cuddled or because of a wet diaper, I felt like she was trying to communicate with me. I just didn't know what she wanted, and therefore I kept asking, "What do you want?" That, I learned later, was the first of many mistakes.

Eventually the behaviors progressed and soon there was no denying it; this was not normal. Before long Abigail was routinely punching her head and nose to the point of making black and blue marks and even drawing blood.

Imagine watching someone hurting herself almost uncontrollably. It was horrific. All I kept thinking was that she must not realize what she was doing; otherwise she wouldn't be doing it, right?

My first instinct, of course, was to protect her. This was my child, for goodness sakes! I told her "No" very sternly, but that made her hit herself more. I held her hand down but when I let it go she would hit herself a hundred times more, with even more intensity. It was unbearable to watch, but if I tried to ignore her, inadvertently holding my breath, she only hit herself harder. What was she trying to say? I begged her to tell me, even though I knew she couldn't talk. I felt completely helpless, and neither Brett nor I had any idea whatsoever how to deal with it.

We hit a wall when we went on vacation for our fourth anniversary. I had hired a babysitter to help my mother take care of Abigail for the three days we were gone. When we returned, we discovered the entire right side of Abigail's face was black and blue. I mean, the entire right side of her face. I had never seen a bruise like that on anyone, and I played softball for ten years and saw tons of black and blue marks. If I didn't know Abigail better I would have thought someone had beaten her. As nauseating as this sounds, it might have been better, because the realization that our two-year-old daughter had done this to herself was almost more than we could bear.

When my husband saw the mark, he immediately asked me to take Abi to the pediatrician to have it documented. We didn't want anyone calling Children Protective Services on us, and since our pediatrician understood the situation, we knew she'd believe us when we told her that Abi had done this to herself. After that trip, we purchased a popsicle-stick splint from a physical therapy catalog and put it on her right arm – the one she used to hit herself – to restrain her every night.

By the time we met Pete, the behavioral psychologist at Kennedy Krieger, we were desperate for help. Pete showed me the floor dedicated to injuriously behaved children and I was disturbed that Abigail was so much younger than the other patients on the floor. Most of them were between ten and eighteen years old. Abigail was only two! Was she going to be locked in a hospital forever?

Some of the kids had restraints on. Some had to be surrounded by a ring of six bodyguards whenever they left their rooms. One kid, a spitter, was guarded by personnel covered in plastic robes and faceguards. Pete even showed me bruises on his arms where he'd been bitten.

I couldn't imagine dealing with this for the rest of Abi's life. I begged Pete for help, but he told me they'd never had a patient as young as Abigail. It would take some doing, but he promised to try to figure out a way for Abigail to enter the program. As you've already read in the previous chapter, he succeeded.

Kennedy Krieger Institute was a turning point in more ways than one. Though our time there didn't actually change Abigail's behaviors significantly (in fact, for a while, the behaviors got worse!), they made *me* better. I finally understood why Abigail was behaving the way she was. I also got a wonderful education in applied behavior analysis (ABA), a way to understand and improve behaviors.

Dozens of books have been written on ABA (see the Resource Guide for specific titles) so I won't go into too much detail, but let me just give you a brief explanation: typical children learn from their environment. They watch those around them and naturally imitate them. Johnny watches his mom vacuum the floor, and when you give Johnny a little vacuum, he vacuums the floor.

Abigail did not pick up cues like a typical child. Give Abi a vacuum and she'd try to eat it. In order for her to learn to use a vacuum, I had to put the vacuum in her hand, push it back and forth, add a vacuum song, and maybe after ten to twenty repetitions she'd be able to push it back and forth herself.

Abigail, I learned, had no idea how to get my attention. Sure, she'd seen people tapping each others' shoulders or calling out to one another, but like the vacuum scenario, she couldn't pick up these social cues on her own. What she had learned was that when she hit herself, she got our attention. What we realized once we started our sessions at Kennedy Krieger was that by giving the behavior attention, Abi kept on doing it. She didn't care what attention it was. Verbal, non-verbal, happy, or angry, all she cared about was that her behaviors got people to look at her. She was using the hitting as a way to communicate and get people's attention, and that had been going on for so long it had become a pattern embedded in her brain.

Now that we'd figured that out, our job was to break the pattern. We would do that by harnessing the power of desire and by properly using rewards. In other words, we'd use something Abi really loved and wanted – such as her mother singing – to motivate her to get my attention appropriately.

Every single day, we went into a padded room to perform "discrete trials." Abigail sat in a cubed chair with Pete behind her and I sat in front with my back to her. Our one and only goal was to teach Abi to get my attention without hitting herself. For four hours a day Pete would say "If you want Mommy, touch her." And she'd hit herself. But this time, I didn't give her the attention she craved. I just sat there with my back to her. Not surprisingly, Abi was unhappy about that. In fact, she was furious. She threw herself on the floor, screamed, and banged on the padded floor. Sometimes she exhausted herself so much she fell asleep. Other than when we were in the room with Pete, Abi wore restraints on both of her arms to keep her from hurting herself.

This also helped me stop reinforcing her bad behavior by giving her attention when she hit. She eventually had to make the connection that when the restraints were off, hitting herself didn't get Mommy's attention.

The first few weeks of this process were emotionally draining, to say the least. I couldn't stand watching Abigail get mad and frustrated. I wanted to hold her, take the pain away, and make her smile. But I knew that she didn't need me to hold her. She needed to get through this awful, terrible stuff in order to stop hitting herself. So I removed the emotional connection and tried to learn as best I could.

My husband, however, could not divorce himself emotionally. The first time he observed he got so mad he walked out of the room and demanded we come home. Did I mention that was the first time he observed? It was also his last. Of course, it wasn't easy for me either. I practically held my breath every time Abi screamed, but after I was finally able to breathe again, I was happy to stay. I was fascinated by how simple the process was and how I hadn't previously seen it, even though it was clear as day.

And then, during week three, she did it. I sat in front of her with my back turned and she reached out and touched me. Immediately I turned around and started singing *Twinkle Twinkle Little Star* with a huge smile on my face. Abigail seemed just as thrilled as I was, but our happiness was short-lived because, unable to connect the dots herself, she couldn't repeat what she'd done. She knew she wanted me to sing, but she didn't know how she'd gotten me to do it the first time so she couldn't get me to do it again. The tantrums began all over again, and this time they were worse! She screamed, hit, bit, and even spit. Things got so bad that Pete had to get her in a bear hold to keep her from hurting herself, him, or me.

Finally, things started to calm down, and toward the end of week four she began to get the concept. Finally she knew that if she touched me, I'd turn around, but she started hitting again anyway because she still connected hitting with getting my attention. To get past this, Pete instructed me to immediately turn back around and ignore Abigail until she touched me again. He had to block her hands at times, but we were determined to help her make the connection that touching me would get her the reward and hitting would get her nothing.

About two weeks later, Abi turned the corner. She touched me, I sang, she touched me again, and I sang again. We continued it over and over, touching and singing, touching and singing, and I was over the moon.

When we felt she was ready, we moved the lessons outside the padded room, touching and singing in the hallway, cafeteria, and various waiting rooms. (I think the hospital staff had to wear ear plugs because I'm no Celine Dion!)

Abigail needed to carry the exercise over to settings other than the padded room and also with people other than me, so we flew my Florida babysitter in, and Brett even came back to do the exercises with us during the last week of the program.

Although Abi was still occasionally hitting herself, by the time we were finished with Pete and the Krieger Institute, we had a new starting point, a turnaround, a new beginning. We had learned that we needed to change our behavior in order to change Abigail's behavior. We realized that Abigail didn't learn like typical children and that she needed things spelled out for her in a systematic way. To put it simply, Abigail's behaviors shouldn't, and couldn't, make us react, because our reactions taught her how to act.

When we got home, we continued the ABA with Kate, a certified ABA therapist, five days a week, two hours a day. Kate also taught us the sister therapy of ABA called AVB, for applied verbal behavior, which focuses on teaching through language.

Keep in mind that language does not necessarily mean speaking. The precursor to language is imitation. Thus, one of the key tools of AVB is imitation. The first hour with Kate was lessons for me, Brett, and our babysitter, then we'd sit with Abigail and apply what we'd learned.

For example, one of our first goals was to get Abigail to communicate "Yes" and "No." At the time, Abigail was hitting herself to communicate every word. In other words, for "Yes" she hit and for "No" she hit too. We sat Abigail down with Kate behind her and a floor full of toys in front of her. Some of the toys she loved; others she didn't care for. I sat near the toys and asked Abi if she wanted a specific toy. When Abigail went to hit herself, Kate blocked her and I put my hand over her hands to give her enough strength to either grab the toy or push it away. Within about two or three months, she finally grasped the concept of "I want" or "I don't want," and then we could move to the next step: shaking her head "Yes" or "No." It took the rest of the year to do this, but finally Abi figured out how to initiate the action of nodding or shaking her head by herself and we only had to remind her verbally, "Tell me yes or no."

Kate worked on many things with us that year. She helped teach Abigail how to point at things that were out of her reach and how to play with toys, such as pushing buttons to activate them or squeezing Elmo to make him laugh. The cause and effect toys were a big hit because Abigail was rewarded immediately for her action – she pushed the button and Elmo spoke. Over time, Abigail also learned how to communicate properly using gestures rather than hitting. She even learned how to live without Mommy for a minute or two if I had to step away.

We were on the right road and there was a light at the end of the tunnel, so much so that we decided to go for another baby (more on that in the next chapter).

We would have loved to have kept Kate forever, but it was becoming very expensive. ABA can cost up to $1,500 a week, so by the time Abigail was about three and a half, we felt we had enough control to handle things ourselves.

Before Kate left, she gave us a behavior protocol. This ten-page report outlined our future goals and what we needed to do to help Abigail reach them, such as blocking the hits and gently redirecting her to a more appropriate behavior or changing our tone of voice. In short, we were instructed to ignore and redirect any inappropriate behaviors. It was tough to do on our own, but we managed, and thank goodness we learned what we did because when our son was born (perfectly healthy, thank goodness), he began to exhibit behavior problems at only a year old, but this time I knew what to do.

When he threw himself on the floor kicking and screaming, I just walked away. I didn't get emotional. In fact, I didn't respond at all because I knew then that inappropriate behaviors do not deserve any attention. Today, I believe you can learn the basics of applied behavior analysis and apply them to any child in any situation. Between you and me, ABA even works on my husband.

Many children with disabilities experience difficulty expressing themselves, which can lead to frustration and further delays in language. I would like to teach you some of the fundamentals of applied verbal behavior because AVB can help any child learn, as I saw from my typically developing son, though it's used mostly these days with children on the autistic spectrum. While Abigail does not have autism, like children on the spectrum, she's unable to pick up cues from her environment, so AVB is a wonderful learning tool for her, too.

Ultimately, we learned that before you can do anything about the behavior you want to change, you need to identify three things: what precedes the behavior, what is the behavior, and what are the consequences of the behavior. (This is called the ABC's, which stand for "antecedent," "behavior," and "consequences.")

Okay, I lied. You do need one more thing: you need to determine what will motivate the person you're working with. Then, if the child taps you, says your name, or does something appropriately, the consequence is the reward. But if the behavior is inappropriate, such as screaming, jumping on furniture, or hitting, make sure the child is safe and ignore the behavior to the best of your ability.

Essentially, you're taking an undesirable behavior and shaping it into one that's more desirable. To reach that goal, things have to be broken down into parts, or sequences. For Abigail, our long-term goal was for her to use her vocal sounds to get people's attention. Once she got that attention and made eye contact, she could use sign language to convey her wants and desires. In order to reach this goal, we had to break it into smaller goals, shaping the behavior with rewards along the way.

As you saw earlier in the chapter, the first mini-goal was to shape the undesirable behavior of hitting herself into a more desirable one: reaching out and touching the person. Once we achieved that goal, we could move to using her voice to get attention.

We also used this process of rewarding good behavior to help Abigail get through things she didn't want to do. For example, Abigail hated doing weight-bearing exercises, so we'd tell her that if she did the wheelbarrow walk for ten minutes, she'd get to play with her favorite musical toy. The most important thing was to find Abi's currency, so to speak – what was important to her – and use it to our advantage.

You're probably thinking "That's bribery!" but I call it positive reinforcement, and reinforcements are especially important for children with special needs. You reward them for their hard work, fade the rewards gradually, and eventually they learn to be proud of their own successes.

Another important concept we learned while teaching Abi is called "prompting," which is really just another word for helping, and it can be both verbal and physical. Prompting helped decrease Abi's frustration while learning something new. For example, I had finally learned that much of Abi's negative behavior stemmed from her inability to communicate, so I had to give her a way to let us know what she needed.

Accordingly, when she was about three and a half, we began to teach her sign language. At first we began to physically help her do the movements ("prompted" her to do them) while verbally telling her the word.

Abigail's first sign was for music, her favorite thing in the world. To help her learn the sign (also considered a "mand" or "request"), we physically made the sign for her by holding one arm straight with her palm up while using the other hand to rub the straight arm up and down. She was rewarded with a song and the connection in her brain was almost instant. She learned that sign in one day.

After a few days, we started fading the prompts, moving to holding only her elbows, and eventually, with time and repetition, not helping her physically at all. We got to the point where we were able to simply say, "Abigail, tell me bed" or "Abigail, tell me music" and she'd perform the sign herself.

One very important thing to note while teaching, shaping, and reinforcing behaviors: it is a team effort and everyone must be on the same page. Imagine three people telling you how to do something three different ways. You would be confused and frustrated. The same concept applies to children. Everyone involved in your child's life – mom, dad, teachers, therapists, etc. – must know what you are working on and exactly how you are doing it and they must do it the same way. Consistency is critical.

Therefore, from the start of Abi's therapy program, we used a daily journal, a short meeting every day, and several multi-hour meetings throughout the year to keep everyone on the same proverbial page. We operated as a school, with me as the director and the others playing the roles of lead teacher and assistants. Every morning my lead teacher and I would meet and discuss our goals and how we were going to reach them. I then passed the information down the line.

No doubt, children's behaviors can be disruptive, embarrassing, frustrating, and depressing to parents. Whether you have a child with screaming tantrums, one who tries to hurt you, or one who is self-injurious, these are children with behaviors of frustration. They are calling for attention. Most children, regardless of their abilities, have a hard time putting words together to express their feelings, wants, and desires. Children with disabilities have an even more difficult time because some are non-verbal, some lack environmentally learned social-emotional skills, and some have language skills that are not fully developed. This is where we can use AVB as a tool to teach communication.

Think about some of the adults you know. Some of them have a difficult time expressing themselves, too. It takes years to learn the art of language and a lifetime to understand how to talk with others.

Today, I have deep compassion for children who can't express themselves for various reasons, but that does not mean I feed their inappropriate behaviors. It is our job as parents to raise and teach our children basic survival skills, and communication is key. Children don't automatically know how to express their feelings. They must be taught, and it is ten times harder for children with disabilities to convey their feelings when communication is naturally difficult for them. Some children even have neurological issues that fight against them in the language processing center of the brain. We need patience when dealing with bad behaviors and teaching language, but knowing what to do and what not to do is critical.

When we finally learned how to deal with Abigail's behaviors and how to help her communicate the best way she could without getting frustrated, our lives literally changed. We transformed Abigail's behaviors through positive reinforcement, which made a world of difference in her life and in ours, too.

5

The Joy
of Siblings

Way back on my first date with Brett, I'd told him I wanted six kids. He'd laughed and said I was crazy but I was steadfast – I was studying to be a doctor and I was on the hunt for my Mr. Mom. He had never been around babies before, but after we'd been dating for a while he was willing to compromise and go for three children.

That all changed when we had Abigail and our lives became consumed with her. In the back of our minds we knew we'd probably eventually try for another child, but we just didn't have the time or energy to think about it yet.

Until September 11, 2001. The day before, my grandfather had passed away. I was making plans to leave Baltimore and fly with Abi back to Florida to be with my family for the funeral when the attacks took place in New York City. Immediately, Baltimore was completely locked down. Tanks littered the streets and F-14s flew through the skies. It was terrifying, and when they cancelled all therapies at the hospital that day, I had nobody to talk to.

I sat upstairs in the playroom at Kennedy Krieger watching the attacks on television, feeling completely alone and sobbing. I couldn't leave the city, I couldn't be with my mom for my grandfather's funeral, my husband was hundreds of miles away, and I wanted desperately to be home, safe and secure with my family. But all the airports and train stations were closed, so Abi and I were trapped in a city in which we knew nobody. Somehow we made it through the day, and after Abigail was asleep, I locked myself in the bathroom and fell to the floor, crying hysterically.

When the airport finally re-opened on September 13, Abigail had only three weeks left to complete the program. Since we were at such a critical point, I decided to stay. It was an eerie feeling living in the city after the attacks. Police stood guard on every corner and my feelings of solitude and desperation grew every day until we finally made it home in October. The moment I landed in Florida, Brett and I embraced to the point of numbness. He drove us home and I knew this was all I wanted, to be safe and sound at home with my family.

Later that week, Brett and I spoke about how I had felt. How I'd had this overwhelming need to be with family, which consisted of myself, Brett, and our daughter Abigail. We started to ask ourselves, "Is this it? Do we want to give Abigail a brother or sister? But in this time of feeling so insecure, do we really want to have another child?"

It was a difficult decision. We knew that at some point Brett and I would be gone, and we didn't want Abigail to be completely alone after that happened. We also thought we should take the opportunity to create another life now before something else happened in the world. Brett and I felt so close during those few months after 9/11 that we didn't want to leave our house. We didn't travel, shop, or attend public events. We stayed home and enjoyed our time together, just the three of us, and we thought long and hard about whether or not we wanted to create another child.

Before we decided yes or no, I also wanted to make sure I would not have another sick child. We got a referral to see a local geneticist and we sat in his office telling him everything about Abigail's unbalanced translocation and my husband's OI. We wanted to make sure that if we had another child, he or she would be healthy, and we were hoping the science was up to date enough to let us do that.

I knew about amniocentesis, which usually happens between sixteen and twenty weeks of pregnancy, but the doctor told me about something I'd never heard of, Chorionic villus sampling (CVS), which is done earlier, between weeks ten and thirteen. In this test, the doctor takes cells from the placenta at the point where it attaches to the uterine wall and the cells are then screened for various genetic abnormalities.

Armed with this new information, Brett and I spent that night talking about our choices. Within a few hours we'd made our decision. We'd roll the dice and gamble, knowing what risks we were taking. The testing would tell us whether or not the child had a genetic abnormality, but there was still the question of what we'd do with that information. I am Catholic, and I knew that terminating a pregnancy is a sin in the eyes of the church, but we simply couldn't handle another sick child.

If we successfully got pregnant, we'd keep it a secret, do the CVS, and deal with the next step as needed. We went to work conceiving and I became obsessed with pregnancy tests. Remember when the doctors weren't sure if I could get pregnant once, let alone twice? Apparently my husband has a gift for making babies. The pregnancy test returned positive in January, 2002.

During my eighth week of pregnancy, I had the CVS procedure. It was a nerve- wracking day and it seemed like everything – the clock in the bathroom, the morning drive to West Palm, sitting in the waiting room, not to mention the actual procedure – moved in slow motion. The moment the needle went into my stomach I felt like time was frozen, or perhaps it was I who was frozen. The procedure took only five minutes but it felt like an hour.

I held my breath the whole procedure, asking for forgiveness for even going through with the test, much less for considering terminating the pregnancy. I lay in bed for the next forty-eight hours to reduce the chance of miscarriage, and over the next seven weeks we kept my growing belly a secret. (Because of the OI, the CVS results took longer than usual to get.)

As time went by the baby grew and even began moving, and I was getting more and more anxious. Was I going to keep this pregnancy or not? It was getting harder and harder to face the decision I might have to make. Once I hit fifteen weeks, I felt there was no turning back. I had been caring for this baby, watching my diet and stress levels, making sure I took my folic acid, and not overdoing things physically. At this point, all I could do was pray, so I did.

Two days after the fifteen-week mark, the phone rang. It was the geneticist's office, who informed us that we had a healthy baby boy. No genetic abnormalities. No OI. I must have asked the nurse "Are you sure?" three times, because I couldn't believe what she'd just told me. I hung up the phone and ran around the house shouting with glee. I called Brett and when I told him, he began to cry. All the boys in his family had OI and he'd never thought a healthy baby boy was possible. But it was, and it looked like we were going to have one. A healthy son we could watch play soccer and baseball, ride a bike, climb on a jungle gym – all the things healthy little boys can do without worrying about breaking a bone. We were ecstatic beyond words.

Once we got that wonderful news, we knew we had a lot of ducks to line up. Abigail was continuing to make tremendous progress, but with the baby on the way she had to learn how to be gentle. We bought bald baby dolls (so she wouldn't eat the hair) and literally walked her step-by-step through how to act with the baby.

First, we placed the baby doll in her arm and kept our hands over her hands showing her how to hold it. Second, we taught her how to stroke the baby with a soft gentle touch using hand over hand again and again. We did these exercises several times throughout the day and continuously praised Abi, telling her how sweet she was. Abigail always loved praise, and it really helped boost her self-confidence.

I knew I'd soon need more help with Abigail. My growing belly was getting in the way and I couldn't lift her or do therapy anymore. Plus, taking care of Abigail, her medications, doctor appointments, therapies, and schooling was a full-time job. How was I going to give her the attention she needed with a newborn latched onto me? I had to find others to help me.

First on my list was a live-in nanny. I interviewed at least a hundred applicants but I just couldn't commit. Nobody seemed like the perfect Mary Poppins I envisioned, and the months flew by without me hiring anyone. In my ninth month I panicked and decided to call a nursing agency for help with Abigail. At that point I just didn't have the time or energy to interview anyone, and I felt that a nurse's aide would be more well-trained than a nanny.

The woman they sent was an angel. My hormones were raging and I acted like a complete lunatic, criticizing everything this poor nurse's aide did from morning till night. Despite that, she stayed on and helped our family for several years.

A week before I was due to give birth, a physical therapy student from Australia called about the nanny job, and called, and called, and called. I had given up looking for a nanny, but this student wouldn't give up. I finally decided to give her an interview and I hired her on the spot. She turned out to be a lifesaver, helping wherever I needed her, and she spent a ton of time taking what she was studying at school and applying it to Abigail, helping her with the skills she'd need to walk one day.

Over my entire pregnancy, I was followed by my regular ob/gyn and also by a high-risk ob because of everything we'd been through. Every week the high-risk ob did an ultrasound to evaluate the baby's size, weight, and functions of all the organs and each week he reassured us that everything was fine. On October 4, 2002, Ethan William Zimmerman, our flawless baby boy, was born. This wonderfully healthy boy was handsome to boot!

During the first few months after Ethan was born, I had to figure out how to balance two demanding children, a husband, a home, and work. I knew by then that the only thing I really could do alone was breastfeeding. For everything else I needed help, but the addition of Ethan to our family...There simply aren't words to convey what he brought to our lives.

Abigail's eyes sparkled whenever Ethan was around. She wanted to hold him, pointing her finger at him and staring at him lovingly. I put her hands under him while I supported his weight and she smiled at him and licked his head – her version of a kiss. The practice we'd done with Abi before Ethan was born paid off. For the most part Abigail was excellent with Ethan, and he was a great sport too.

After only a few weeks I had this two-kid thing down pat. During the days, Abigail and I played with toys while Ethan sat in his bouncy seat. When evening came we went outside and played on the swings tied to our big oak tree or I pulled the kids around the neighborhood in their little red wagon. When the neighbors came out to say hello, you could see that Abigail was so proud, looking at Ethan, then back at the neighbors. You could almost hear the words "Look at my brother" coming out of her mouth.

As Ethan and Abigail grew, I tried to have them do as much together as possible. For a time they were very close in age developmentally so they enjoyed doing many of the same things throughout the day. Ethan participated in Abi's therapy, whether it was doing sit ups on the physio-ball, balancing on a platform swing, finger painting with food condiments, or manipulating thera-putty.

I loved how protective Abigail was over Ethan, though it became troublesome when his crying upset her. During the times that Ethan was teething, I actually had to separate them because he cried so much that she couldn't handle it. But all in all, juggling the two kids was manageable, even though the beds went unmade during many of those early days and I don't even want to think about the dust bunnies underneath them.

A messy house was worth it when we realized how much the baby was teaching Abigail. As the months went on, Ethan began hitting milestone after milestone, some earlier than usual, and Abigail watched him in amazement. I could almost see the word bubble appearing over her head, "How did he do that? Can I do it too?"

Amazingly, she'd try to imitate him, holding her hands a certain way with a toy, or moving her tongue and lips the way his did when he ate. We had worked so hard on teaching Abigail how to imitate with the behavior therapist Kate, but we hadn't gotten nearly as far as we'd wanted to. But here we were, a few months later, and Abigail was imitating spontaneously thanks to her baby brother.

Best of all, right after Ethan began to crawl, Abigail figured out to frog hop around the room. She put her hands on the floor and scooted her butt and both of her knees closer to her hands, almost like a leap. The first time Brett and I saw her do it next to Ethan, we jumped up and down like crazy people, telling them "Go, go, go!" like they were dashing for the finish line of *The Amazing Race*.

After that we started deliberately placing toys and Ethan's binky out of their reach so they would have to race to get them. Although Ethan always won, that didn't stop us from cheering them both on, and losing didn't seem to damper Abi's spirits. She continued to race next to him over and over.

We were overjoyed. This family entertainment night after night was the best show ever, and we couldn't believe how happy we all were. Ethan had effortlessly accomplished something we hadn't been able to do in two years of trying. He was inspiring Abigail to imitate spontaneously. We never imagined that having another child would act as a role model for Abi, but that was exactly what was happening. Everything Ethan did, Abigail wanted to try. Sometimes her physical limitations and muscle tone held her back, but we were right there to help if needed.

Ironically, Abi's little brother turned out to be her big brother, teaching her everything he knew. The first year flew by and it was relatively easy. When Ethan began to walk at age one, it was difficult to see how desperately Abigail wanted to imitate him. We bought her a walker that she wasn't quite ready for but I stressed to the therapist that our goal was to get her to walk. Today she does use the walker with some assistance steering, but she still wants to run like her brother.

A few years later Ethan started asking questions. "Why can't Abi run or talk?" I told him, "Abi isn't as strong as you are." And every year since I have been telling him more and more about Abigail based on his level of comprehension.

I know some day when Ethan grows up he will thank Abi for teaching him, too. She teaches him understanding and compassion for others. I hear from the babysitters that when Brett and I are not around he is very protective of her. He makes sure that she is never left out and receives all the attention she needs.

Recently, his school teachers told me that Ethan talks about his sister all the time and teaches his peers sign language. Abigail will always play a special part in his life, and not a day goes by that I'm not grateful Brett and I made the decision to give Abigail a sibling, and ourselves another child.

6

Be Your
Own Doctor

*T*he first three and half years of Abigail's life were spent in and out of hospitals and doctors' offices and in endless therapy sessions. While I hadn't become the medically certified Dr. Zimmerman I had once hoped to be, I had, in a sense, become a doctor nonetheless. I was Dr. Mom to Abigail. I had learned medication names, doses, uses, and interactions. As Abigail collected diagnoses like stickers from each specialist – hypotonic, failure to thrive, oral dysphasia, nystagmus, delayed gastric emptying, myoclonic seizures, tonic-clonic seizures, intrauterine growth retardation – I found myself talking in medical terminology rather than layman's terms. If a new doctor asked what medications Abi was on, I answered in doctor-ese, rattling off milligrams, concentrations, and even saying "BID" instead of "twice a day."

Over the years I had also become an expert on specialists. I knew most of the neurologists, cardiologists, gastroenterologists, and urologists in the tri-county area. I learned who had good bedside manners and who didn't, who had an aggressive approach and who was more conservative. I knew who liked to hand out medications, who you had to beg for a prescription, and who told you your child was going to be like a monkey. As you probably guessed, I never went back to Dr. Bedside Manners at the University of Miami, and yes, he was a…

Well, I'm a lady, so I'll just call him a cad, but I learned from that cad. After that day, I didn't walk into just any doctor's office. I looked for a doctor who spent time getting to know Abigail's medical history and who asked us questions. Since Abigail has so many diagnoses, every doctor who sees her must take into account all of her problems. They must see her as a whole child, not just an eye, a kidney, or a stomach.

For instance, we went through four gastroenterologists before we finally found one we liked. The day we met her, she spent an entire hour asking questions about Abigail, Brett, and me. By the end of our appointment, I felt like she knew Abi well enough to make medical decisions for her. The best part of the story? The next time we saw her, a full six months later, she remembered everything we had told her. Now that's a good specialist.

Another key ingredient I now look for in a specialist is good eye contact, which shows me the doctor is listening and has compassion for you and your child. He's actually making a connection as opposed to just checking off yet another chart. I remember Dr. Bedside Manners never made eye contact until my husband started yelling…I guess that got his attention.

The final thing on my checklist these days is a doctor who returns phone calls. When you have a child with special needs you may be calling at all hours with concerns and you may also need continuous medication refills. After seeing one neurologist for a little over a year, Abigail had a break-through seizure again. The doctor's office was closed, so I left a detailed message on the answering machine. I left another message with the receptionist the next morning, then another message later in the day after no return phone call. Believe it or not, an entire week went by with no return call! My pediatrician tried to help too but got nowhere. In the meantime, we were petrified Abigail was going to have another seizure. When she did a few weeks later, we immediately searched for a new specialist. I wasn't about to jeopardize Abigail's health because a doctor was too busy to take care of all her patients.

A good doctor should also be willing to help you with financial concerns, like fighting with insurance companies and Medicaid to pay for a certain drug or other special needs. When Abigail was a year and a half old, her gastroenterologist fought hard with the insurance company to cover her special amino acid diet. She wrote letters and even called the insurance company to explain why they should pay for it. In the end, they denied us and I had to pay out of pocket, but it wasn't for lack of trying on Abi's doctor's part!

When Abi's doctor wrote a prescription for a drug like Prevacid instead of Nexium, she also wrote a letter to the insurance company explaining why she wrote the script for that particular drug, since insurance companies rarely pay in full for certain name-brand drugs.

Recently, our GI had to write a medical necessity letter for Abi's feeding tube. Typically, insurance companies pay for a new one every three months, but since Abigail needs a new one every month, the doctor wrote a letter stating Abi has a history of bacteria overgrowth, which can cause infection in the tube. Just like that, we now have a new feeding tube, paid in full by our insurance company, every month.

A few times, I truly did assume the role of Dr. Mom. Better than a paper degree, I had a mother's instinct, which I relied upon to literally save Abigail's life. One of the first times was when Abigail was about a year old. She had the flu with a high fever and she couldn't stay hydrated, throwing up fluids faster than I could get them in her. For two nights in a row I took her to the emergency room, and the same doctor hydrated her with IV fluids, then sent us home even after I explained that she couldn't hold down fluids.

On day three I'd had enough. I stood in the middle of the emergency room and firmly told this doctor (okay, I was screaming at the top of my lungs) that I was not leaving the ER until he admitted us upstairs. It couldn't look good on his shift that the same patient had returned three times for the same reason, so he finally gave in and admitted her.

Abigail spent a week in the hospital getting IV fluids, and we had peace of mind that our daughter wouldn't suffer from dehydration (or worse) at home anymore.

Dr. Mom kicked in again a few months later when Abigail started exhibiting strange symptoms at home. One afternoon I was sitting at the kitchen table with Abigail on my lap. Brett came home from work and when he walked over to say hello, Abigail's eyes widened, she began to tremble, and then she screamed bloody murder.

I managed to calm her down, figuring it was just a fluke, but then it happened again and again that week – she'd be completely calm, then out of the blue she'd completely flip out. My mother's intuition told me something wasn't right, so I took her to the pediatrician. She examined her and couldn't see anything wrong, but she was concerned enough to send us to the emergency room for an MRI.

The test showed nothing abnormal, and after an hour of monitoring in the ER, the doctors sent us home, telling us they couldn't find anything amiss. When we returned to the ER two more times that month they insisted there was nothing wrong with Abigail and sent us on our way. Finally, Brett and I began to doubt ourselves. Perhaps we were just imagining this, but then it would happen again. One minute she'd be completely fine, then she'd let out a blood-curdling scream and nothing could calm her down.

Day after day I searched for help, seeing the pediatrician on call, investigating on the internet, calling various specialists. Then, finally, we found a neurologist who believed us. He speculated that one of her medications was making her hallucinate, like being on a bad mushroom trip. He admitted us to the hospital for observation in the intensive care unit, and after witnessing what we had been seeing, he changed her seizure medication.

Immediately Abi's outbursts stopped, and I no longer felt like a crazy person. (I have to admit there was more than one time I thought perhaps I was a lunatic.) Indeed, I learned my lesson: if you feel like you aren't getting answers, keep searching. I'm Abi's mother. I know her best. If it walks like a duck and talks like a duck, it's a bad seizure medication trip!

By far the hardest medical stay was when Abigail was three and I had just become pregnant with Ethan. Her gums began to bleed randomly and she developed some nasty sores in her mouth. I took her to an oral surgeon, who agreed to monitor her for a few days and if necessary perform surgery to remove the sores. Coincidentally, a week after the sores showed up in her mouth, she started to grimace in pain if we asked her to put weight on one foot. Within a few weeks she began crying every time she had to put her leg down, so we took her to an orthopedist, who admitted her to the hospital to rule out infection in the joints.

X-rays and MRIs showed nothing wrong, but Abigail's pain continued to get worse and soon she could no long bear weight on either leg. By week two of her hospital stay, she was paralyzed in pain and I had to beg for stronger pain medication for her. For an entire week she lay in bed, covered in soft cotton padding to keep her from moving. By week three I couldn't even change her diaper, she was in such pain. The hospital called consults from every specialty – oncology, infectious disease, neurology, gastroenterology, etc. They performed two nuclear body scans, more MRIs, bone biopsies, and blood work up the ying yang.

At one point the infectious disease doctor hinted that she might have leukemia and I had the breakdown of all breakdowns. Were we finally going to lose her? How long could she suffer like this? I cried like a baby for my little girl.

The nights were torture. I was the only one there to care for her in the middle of the night as she cried in pain, looking at me with her puppy dog eyes. Although she never uttered a word, I felt like she was pleading with me for help. I had to change her diaper two to three times a night to avoid diaper rash and urinary track infections, and it nearly killed me to inflict pain on her by moving her around.

Whenever Brett or my mom came to visit Abigail, I went to the medical library. I searched for research or articles on sudden acute bone pain on Medline, but like the doctors, I couldn't find a diagnosis.

It was during this horrendous time that I came to an epiphany of sorts. I was in the car, driving to my sister's house to take a shower and a nap while my mom stayed in the hospital with Abi. While I drove, I turned on the radio and the song "Hero" by Enrique Inglesias started playing. It was currently at the top of the charts, and as I listened to the lyrics I began to sob so hard I had to pull the car over.

I suddenly realized that all that mattered was Abigail's happiness without pain and suffering. It was okay if she was disabled, labeled mentally retarded, and needed lifelong care. As long as she never had to suffer again like she currently was, it would be okay. If she could just make it through whatever this was, we would figure out how to go forward.

Finally, one week later, the radiologist diagnosed Abigail with periostitis, a painful inflammation around the bones. Why did she have this? The doctors suspected scurvy, a disease that results from insufficient intake of vitamin C. They gave her megadoses of the vitamin and almost immediately she was cured.

I felt like whacking myself in the head like the guy in the V-8 commercial. After five weeks of torture, all Abigail needed was a couple of glasses of orange juice?

Suddenly, Abigail was a celebrity. Her room was a revolving door of doctors and medical students coming to get a look at the little girl with scurvy, a disease no one had seen in decades.

The doctors and I went over her daily diet to try to figure out why she wasn't getting enough Vitamin C. When we calculated it all out, it became clear that Abigail wasn't absorbing the nutrients from her food properly. The next step, said her doctors, was to find out why.

This was the point at which I needed to draw the line. Our family could not keep living in hospitals like this, running test after test, searching for answers that seemed to constantly elude us. This was at least our 500th stay in the hospital. We had spent every Thanksgiving and two birthdays in the hospital. We had tortured our daughter enough.

She didn't absorb nutrients properly? We'd give her extra supplements. She had seizures? We'd give her medications to control them. Sure, every issue that came up could be addressed with more procedures and more tests, but giving a name, a diagnosis, a reason for the problems wasn't going to change anything. We had enough answers to take care of her, and for now, that was enough.

Abigail was the only person in the world with her exact genetic problem, and after three years of the roller coaster, we were ready to let Abigail be Abigail. We didn't need to have all the answers; we needed to move forward.

From that point on, I began to keep daily logs on what went in and out of Abi, just like they had in the hospital. I calculated calories on every drink, snack, baby food jar, and home-cooked meal. I kept track of how much protein she took in as well as her calcium, fruits, vegetables, fats, and sugars. If something seemed off, I did my own research.

And it worked. When I played my daughter's own doctor, I was able to help. Soon after the scurvy episode, I noticed that Abigail was not waking up until 9:00 in the morning, but by 11:00 a.m. she already needed a nap. She'd sleep for an hour, get up, then go down again at 2:30. That nap would last until 4:00 p.m., yet she'd be ready for bed for the night at 7:00 p.m. I began researching the side effects of all the medications she was on and I noticed that her seizure medication listed dizziness, blurred vision, dry mouth, drowsiness, clumsiness, and nausea.

Abigail had most, if not all, of these. For goodness sake, she needed a new seizure medication. I called the neurologist and explained my concerns and we switched Abigail's medications slowly so there wouldn't be any further side effects. After a month, Abigail was more alert than ever.

With everything I'd been through in Abigail's three years of life, I had gained an enormous amount of knowledge. I'd read books, spoken to doctors, and scoured reliable sites on the internet, so much so that I had control of the situation and felt comfortable in taking care of Abigail.

We were even finally able to manage the common cold without emergency care, though we still saw our specialists every six months to a year. I'm not anti-doctor and I don't want to give anyone the impression that I am, but for the next six years we only had to go to the hospital twice.

Finally, we weren't living at a hospital. We weren't probing for more answers to Abigail's problems. We were no longer asking why Abigail was the way she was; we just encouraged her to be all that she could be.

These days, my family and friends call me Dr. Mom and I humbly accept the title. For Abigail, I have to be Dr. Mom. My life-long dream was to care for others, to study the human body and diseases, and in a strange way my dreams have come true.

7

Learning the Ins and Outs of the School System

The Individuals with Disabilities Education Act (IDEA) is a law ensuring services to children with disabilities throughout the United States. From birth to age three, infants and toddlers with disabilities and their families receive early intervention services under IDEA Part C. After age three and through age twenty-one, children and youth receive special education and related services under IDEA Part B.

Part C, which we had been under for the last three years, requires "to the maximum extent appropriate to the needs of the child, early intervention services must be provided in natural environments, including the home and community settings in which children without disabilities participate." In other words, when she was little, Abigail's services were provided either at home or in a therapy center.

Part B, on the other hand, says that state programs need to provide a free appropriate public education in the least restrictive environment for children with disabilities ages three through twenty-two. Students with a disability should have the opportunity to be educated with non-disabled peers to the greatest extent possible and they should have access to the general education curriculum, extracurricular activities, or any other program that non-disabled peers would be able to access, within reason.

In other words, once Abigail turned three, it was time for her to go to school.

I was excited, but also scared at the thought of her venturing into a school setting. Because of all her health problems, including seizures, the feeding tube, and a demanding medication schedule, her immune system was very fragile and I was petrified she might relapse once she was exposed to other children.

I was also worried about losing the intimate relationship I had with Abi and her therapists. In early intervention, I had a lot of control. I chose the therapists, set the appointments, and when Abi was too sick or too tired, I was able to decide whether to go or skip therapy that day.

Part B was completely different. The IDEA Part B is implemented by the school board on a state and local level so my day-to-day involvement, and my decision-making power, would be far less than I was accustomed to.

I knew it was crucial to continue Abi's therapy and I wanted her to start school, so we began the transition process when Abigail was two and a half years old. We got her evaluated, took the psychological tests, and filled out all the forms. Then, toward the end of the process, Abi ended up in the hospital with scurvy.

When I told the transition coordinator that Abi was very sick and I didn't know if she would be able to finish the process, let alone go to school, she told me about something called Hospital Homebound, a nationwide program for medically fragile children who either can't attend school at all or who will be temporarily unable to attend school for more than ten consecutive days.

We thought this sounded promising, so after leaving the   hospital we filled out yet more forms, got her doctors to sign off, and scheduled Abi for special education one hour twice a week, plus physical, occupational, and speech therapy for one hour once a week. It was perfect: we sold the pool table and transformed the living room into Abi's classroom/gym.

Things started off really well. Two mornings a week, Abigail's new teacher, Ms. Peggy, arrived with her bag of tricks – music, puppets, toys, books, and the kitchen sink. She started every lesson with her upbeat music, getting Abi moving and grooving. She worked on teaching Abi the days of the week, routines, colors, and listening skills by telling interactive stories like *The Three Little Pigs* and *Little Red Riding Hood*. Abigail sat on the floor with me behind her clapping her hands and patting her legs. Some days Ms. Peggy would put on a puppet show while Abigail watched in amazement. Or maybe it was confusion. Or maybe both.

One thing was for sure – Abigail loved school. She loved the one-on-one attention and for the most part she was an angel student. Her self-injurious behaviors had all but disappeared and she only hit herself occasionally if she was sick and didn't want to sit for school that day.

Ms. Peggy, Ms. Mary (Abigail's school board-appointed speech therapist), and I worked on goals that would meet her needs during her everyday life, like good eye contact, following objects, and engaging in conversations with body and sign language. Just like I had when Abi was in early intervention, I learned from these therapists and continued working on Abigail's goals every day and night.

I felt I had a good grasp of how children develop and how to promote development through different activities. I called on my experience in high school, when I had volunteered in a preschool classroom, organizing and implementing themes and activities for twenty four-year-olds. Later, I'd taken child development courses with the director of the school and I'd continued to study child development in college.

Since Abigail was no typical three-year-old, Ms. Peggy and Ms. Mary taught me how to break lessons down to the most basic level. Abigail's skills ranged from a three-month-old to a nine-month-old level. She still didn't know how to play with toys or stack blocks, let alone recite her ABC's or pick out colors.

When Abi began school, I was also three months pregnant with Ethan and I wasn't sure how I was going to handle it all, so we placed an ad in the paper with the title "Personal Care Assistant Needed." I didn't know exactly what I wanted, but since Abigail really needed help taking care of herself during the day (I had the nurse's aide to help me with her bath, diaper changes, feedings through the G-tube, and so on at night), I knew I needed more than just a babysitter. Between Brett working a lot, my growing belly, and my own exhaustion, we simply needed more help.

After hundreds of interviews with nannies, nurses, teachers, and grandmas, I got a call from Bonnie. She had just graduated with an elementary education teaching degree but didn't want to teach in the school system because she'd heard there was a lot of politics in our local public schools. Bonnie also had a developmentally delayed niece who used a g-tube, so she had relevant experience.

When she showed up for her interview, I felt an instant connection, and she even returned later that evening to get more face-to-face time with Abigail. The minute they saw each other again they both lit up with genuine smiles and laughs. The interview lasted a few hours, but it flew by like it was minutes. I hired Bonnie immediately and soon she became Abigail's private teacher, caregiver, and more importantly, my mini-me.

All of the other teachers and therapists quickly grew fond of Ms. Bonnie, taking her under their wing and teaching her how to continue Abi's progress when they weren't present. Kate, the behavior specialist, was also with us at that time, working from 4:00 p.m. to 6:00 p.m.

Monday through Friday. It was important that everything the therapists taught Abi be carried over when they weren't there. It was our job to keep up with the goals we had for Abigail, like learning to walk, talk, eat, and have fun. We also worked on pre-pre-pre-kindergarten skills, which a lot of us take for granted. How do you hold blocks? How do you stack blocks? How do you turn pages of a book? How do you move your body to music or clap your hands? What do simple commands like "take" and "give" mean?

Bonnie was a natural with Abigail, and before we knew it "Ms. Bonnie" grew into "Aunt Bonnie." She was part of the family, playing an instrumental role in Abigail's progress. One day I came home from a doctor's appointment and found them painting paper plates. I looked at the colored paints scattered across my kitchen table, crinkled my nose, and asked, "What are you doing?"

"I'm teaching Abigail her colors," Bonnie told me boldly. I'd already seen the other teachers try to teach Abi her colors, so I laughed inside and wished her luck. But sure enough, a few months later, Abigail had learned her colors, thanks to Bonnie and her incessant painting projects. (My kitchen table didn't survive, but it was worth it!)

Another time, when Abi was three and a half and Bonnie had been with us for about six months, Bonnie told me, "I'm putting Abigail on the toilet and we are going to potty train her."

I looked at her with a baffled look and asked, "How are you going to do that? How is she going to tell you she has to go?" Abigail still wasn't speaking and she had only learned a few simple signs, certainly not enough to tell someone she needed to go to the bathroom.

Bonnie's answer? "I don't know but I'll put her on and see what happens."

Funny enough, the little booger peed the very first time we put her on the toilet, and later that day too. Bonnie was right. We made it up as we went along. The first thing we did was make up a schedule. A few times a day, at the same times every day, we'd give her fluids through the g-tube. Forty-five minutes later we'd put her on the potty and sing potty songs while signing "toilet" in sign language. We'd show Abigail how to move her fingers and arm to make the sign, and we'd do it over and over again, hour after hour, every time singing and dancing to reward every tinkle or plop.

About two weeks later, Abigail spontaneously signed "toilet" to us. We screamed and ran to the potty and she peed! We continued our progress, and to this day Abi is potty trained with a combination of the schedule plus signs whenever she has to go at other times.

I recently asked Bonnie what she remembers most about working with Abi in the beginning. She said, "Sitting outside on a blanket after swinging on the swings. Abigail and I were like two little girls giggling and talking volumes with body language, eye movement, and sign language. She seemed to understand everything that day. I just lost myself in her having fun."

Bonnie is still with us, many years later, and I am thankful each day that I have her in our lives. I don't believe I could have physically, mentally, or emotionally taught Abigail completely by myself. There is just too much to worry about and accomplish for one person, and Bonnie has been the other hands and mind that have kept me sane.

All told, our first year with Hospital Homebound was amazing. Abi was making progress. She finally knew her colors, she was manipulating toys, and she was turning hard pages in a book. She was able to make eye contact and she stayed engaged in structured activities. She was becoming aware of her surroundings and she was following one-step commands like "put in" or "give." We had a nice team of teachers and therapists; the only thing missing was other kids. At this point, we felt that Abigail's immune system was stronger and that she could handle a school setting, at least part time. Since she had really only socialized with adults, I felt it was important for her to be with other children at least some of the time.

While it all sounded nice in theory, when we began to look at schools, we realized the reality was very sad. Although there are three elementary schools within our district, the school board wouldn't let us enroll Abigail in those, claiming they weren't equipped to handle her needs. Instead, they wanted her to go to a state-agency school about twenty minutes away.

When I went to visit the school I was disappointed. I saw no genuine interactions – nobody encouraged the children to engage with each other and the teachers hardly interacted with the students. Instead, they moved through the schedule like robots, interrupted only by behavior problems that in my opinion were not properly addressed.

We had a bad feeling about this school, but the board was set on it since it was the only place staffed with a nurse and occupational, physical, and speech therapists. I eventually broke after two meetings and told them we would try it on a part-time basis. Because I was terrified of losing all the gains we'd made in Abi's behavior, I insisted on behavior training for the teachers working with her. I even invited them to our home to train them myself, so we could be in a controlled environment with no distractions.

The protocol seemed pretty straightforward to me. It included not allowing Abigail's hands to touch her head and face and instead taking her hands slowly downward while continuing to engage in the activity.

I worked with the teachers for two days, about three hours each day. I would have liked more time with them, but this was all the school allowed them outside the classroom. When our time was up, I hoped they at least understood the basics – to not reinforce the bad behavior and instead to redirect Abi.

Since Abigail was entitled to a shadow – an aide who would be in the classroom one-on-one just for her – Brett and I begged the committee to hire Bonnie for that position. They denied our request, even after we offered to pay Bonnie's salary ourselves and donate computers. Instead, they hired someone who had no formal training and limited experience. At the very least, we asked them to let us observe to make sure the shadow was following the correct behavior protocol. They refused, but after three more meetings the school finally granted us thirty days of observation.

I'm grateful we got that, because what I saw was both enlightening and horrifying. One autistic child was acting out by screaming and thrashing in the classroom. The solution to his outbursts was to send him and an aide out to the playground. While he was pulling a wagon around and around in circles – which was obviously calming for him but taught him nothing – his aide sat in the corner, talking on her cell phone.

A few days later another boy was banging on the computer, obviously unable to understand how the computer worked. Instead of helping him, the teacher, who was in a closet getting supplies, yelled at him to stop. She continued to yell "Stop!" over and over, without ever leaving the supply closet. Eventually the boy stopped "playing" on the computer and wandered over to bang on a stack of blocks. It broke my heart because he was getting nothing out of his day there. The computer could have been a great resource for him, but he wasn't given the chance.

The most upsetting incident happened a few weeks later. A girl in a wheelchair, who must have been about seven or eight years old, was extremely upset about something. I didn't see what prompted her crying, but it was very loud and very obvious and not one teacher attended to her. Nobody gave her a tissue, nobody tried to find out what was wrong, nobody consoled her. They simply ignored her for at least thirty minutes. I had to hold myself back from marching in and hugging her, but I couldn't compromise my position. I knew if I disrupted the classroom in any way, the school board would have a field day with me, so I just sat there with a knot in my stomach.

I tossed and turned every night, hoping I was doing the right thing for Abi by sending her there. I knew she needed to be around other kids, but was this the environment she was going to thrive in? Since Abigail had the shadow, I knew she was at least getting one-on-one attention, but I still wasn't sure about the decision I'd made.

After a few weeks, it became clear this school wasn't the right choice. Abigail's self-injurious behaviors were returning, so I pulled her out. I decided to continue with the Hospital Homebound program for the remainder of the year, knowing we'd revisit the issue before Abi went to kindergarten.

The next year, we met again with the school board to decide what to do about kindergarten. Should we continue with Hospital Home-bound or try for another school? The board had already made the decision: Abi would go to an out-of-the-house school and they told us about three schools they felt were equipped for Abigail. All had speech, physical, occupational, and behavior therapists as well as a nurse and a one-on-one aide.

Because Abigail was now five years old, she qualified for a "Complex Place Classroom" in the local elementary schools as opposed to the preschool setting she'd required before. This was why, instead of only one school, the school board now had three schools to recommend.

The first name on the list was the state agency school Abi had already attended. Needless to say, we crossed that one off right away, but we agreed to visit the two other schools.

We went in with open minds but were unimpressed with either school. We decided to do our own research and visited elementary schools with Complex Place Classrooms surrounding our district. We were thrilled when we found one we loved, but the district liaison told us it was out of boundaries. Since there were three schools within our district, they wouldn't send Abi to an outside school. My husband fought hard, pretty much begging them to send her to that school, but they wouldn't budge. It was one of the three they chose or none.

At another meeting, I asked if we could do part-time schooling and part-time Hospital Homebound, but they denied that too, saying that Abigail was healthy enough to go to a regular school at this point.

At yet another meeting I told them that if Abi had to go to one of those schools, at the very least they needed to provide an aide who had the proper behavior training. When the board said they'd make no guarantees, I became more and more frustrated.

Before my next meeting, some friends advised me to take a tape recorder so I could have a record of everything everyone said and so that nothing could be misconstrued. I also brought a parent advocate (a parent who is knowledgeable about the law who has been through this process) to assist me, but none of it helped. The board continued to limit our school choices. Most importantly, they couldn't guarantee a behavior specialist or nurse on staff full time, and I left crying my eyes out.

The next step, I learned, was an attorney. After all we'd been through – the many sleepless nights and nail-biting meetings – I decided I couldn't fight anymore. It was just too stressful, so I made the decision to go another way. Brace yourself: you're about to find out just how crazy I really am.

Over the years, therapists and teachers had jokingly referred to my home as "The Zimmerman School House." Everyone was always amazed at how organized, focused, and successful we were. Bonnie and I would put monthly themes together and write goals for Abigail. We decorated the classroom seasonally, with decorations hanging from the ceiling and bulletin boards all done up to match. We created a schedule of morning activities like getting dressed, eating, school time, music time, etc. At the appropriate times, Abigail would go to her schedule and match a duplicated picture to the schedule in order.

Most people knew of my love for children like Abigail because I often spoke to families about various issues. I enjoyed being supportive and talking, giving referrals, or sometimes just being a sounding board. Bonnie and others often said, "You should start your own school," and after hearing it so many times and then striking out so horribly with the school board, I began to think that maybe I should.

I started researching and putting together a business plan. In 2003, only a few months after our last school board meeting, I began the process of incorporating a school. An attorney and I drafted an article of corporation (a fancy name for the legal description listing the board and agents) and later, bylaws for a non-profit organization so we could help other families. After we became a corporation, I developed a business plan, mission statement, objectives, and a course of action (how I'd implement the plan), and I contacted the department of education in Tallahassee to become a certified school.

Next I created a budget of start-up expenses, yearly expenses, competitive salaries (according to the Broward County Salary Schedule), and possible income. Since my husband had agreed to invest some of our own money in order to get the school off the ground, I needed his blessing as well.

I looked at other schools and with a pencil, ruler, and legal pad drew building layouts, picturing what I'd want in my child's school including indoor gyms, group spaces, and also plenty of private spaces for kids to work on their individual goals.

In 2005, I took the director's certificate course at the local college (a requirement to become certified as a director of a school), which helped me organize a parent handbook, personnel handbook, and other important and necessary forms.

We knew there was a need in the area, and we asked local therapy centers to spread the word. It took us another six months to put together the non-profit application and a year for the paperwork to be approved.

In 2007, we began looking for money. We contacted friends, family, friends of friends, friends of family, families of friends, and plenty of local business owners. We told them our story and everyone loved the idea and pledged money to help us.

Once we got the financing, we began to look for a location. We looked at hundreds of buildings and finally decided on a modest space of thirty-three hundred square feet located in a small strip center. The price was right and the lease holders were supportive.

In 2008, The Zimmerman School House, a private non-profit school to help Abigail and other families, finally opened. This facility welcomes children who are moderately to severely disabled. We focus on life skills, therapy, school-readiness skills, communication, and social/emotional skills.

In the state of Florida, a scholarship program helps students with disabilities attend private school. Through our fundraising and corporate donations, we are able to give families a certain additional amount of private school tuition relief. I am thrilled we can offer this type of program for children in our area, and I hope there are similar schools in yours.

If you are not receiving adequate services through your public school district, research whether or not your state will pay for private education. Contact your state or local department of education to learn about your options. The Individual Disability Education Act entitles your child to a free, appropriate education and I encourage you to learn more about this act to give your child what he or she needs and deserves. Remember, your child's needs dictate the services and programs they receive. If you feel you are not getting what you need from your local school board, find a local advocate to help you through the ensuing process. This means a lot of research, but it can be done. (See the Resource Guide for more information.)

Simultaneously, as we worked to get our school up and running, Bonnie and I worked with Abigail from morning to night on everything from colors and the alphabet to talking and walking. We were, and are, an amazing team. We discuss everything regarding Abigail's lessons, behaviors, consistencies, inconsistencies, and long-term goals. It has been wonderful to work with a partner who only has one main focus – Abi's progress. There is no fighting for what is best. We know what is best and we do it, but not everyone can afford this. Therefore, I'm hoping The Zimmerman School House, also known as Abi's Place, can give other families the headache-free education their special-needs children deserve without having to hire their own private teacher.

8

Making
Your Marriage Work

*W*hether you have a child with special needs, five typical children, or no children at all, marriage isn't easy. It requires effort to not take each other for granted, and keeping the connection alive doesn't happen on its own.

I've heard many experts say that the divorce rate is higher among couples who have children with disabilities, and I don't doubt it. Having a child with special needs makes everything harder. We have extra emotional stress, distractions, and financial burdens that other couples never have to deal with. In the past twelve years my marriage has gone through bumps, valleys, and even exhilarating mountain climbs, but so far we've managed to keep it together.

This chapter is extremely personal for me, even more personal than my stories about raising Abigail, but I've forced myself to write this chapter because I feel that sharing my story might help you, if and when you find yourself picking up the phone to call a divorce lawyer.

Okay, let's go back a while. Brett and I first met in 1994 when my sister Nicole and I went to ladies night at a local dance club. I was only eighteen years old, but like most people my age at the time, I had a fake ID so getting into the club wasn't a problem. Brett was Nicole's new boss, and earlier that day at work she'd mentioned that she was going out that night. He said he was going club hopping too and maybe he'd see her out and about. When Nicole saw her boss at the club, she introduced me to him. I was friendly but not overly so. In fact, I was a little miffed. We were there to dance and have fun. This was supposed to be a girls' night out, but whatever.

Brett tried to impress me, buying me flowers and a teddy bear from a vendor working at the club. He bought us drinks too, which I thanked him for, but I wasn't interested in meeting anyone so I continued hanging out with Nicole and dancing.

To this day I blame the DJ for Brett and me getting together, because all of a sudden a great Donna Summer song came out of the speakers and when Brett again asked me to dance, I couldn't turn him down.

Brett told me I had great eyes and that he loved the outfit I was wearing, but I kept dancing, ignoring his flirtation. When the night was over, he walked us out to the car and asked to see me again.

I tried to let him down as nicely as I could, telling him that I was in school full-time and working three jobs. I just didn't have any free time to date, but perhaps I would call him when my schedule freed up.

For the next few days my sister hounded me to go out with him, telling me what a nice guy he was and how he was practically begging her to get me to call him. A few days later one of my jobs called and said they didn't need me that night, so I thought about it, figured he was kind of cute on the dance floor, and decided to give him a try. I called my sister at work and asked her if Brett wanted to take me to dinner.

In a matter of minutes Brett called to formally ask for a date. Rumor has it he actually jumped up and did a little jig, ran to get his car cleaned, got a hair cut, dressed and showered, and picked up two dozen roses all before showing up at my house at 7:00 that night.

The restaurant was beautiful. We sat on the dimly lit patio, looking out onto the water as the evening breeze flowed through our hair. Two hours of talking and eating led to another restaurant, where we enjoyed after-dinner cocktails while rotating 360 degrees every hour for varying views of the ocean. And while the romantic settings sure didn't hurt, what really made the evening was my conversation with Brett. It was just one of those nights when everything clicked. We talked so much that by the end of the night we realized we'd hardly eaten or drunk a thing. Every word that came out of his mouth was exactly what I was going to say, and I know it sounds cheesy, but I felt like I'd found my soul mate.

I know, I know. I was really busy in school, I had those three jobs, and I'd told him I had no time for dating. All of that was totally true. A relationship was the last thing I was looking for, but in spite of all that, I couldn't help myself. I fell in love. Brett and I dated for two months and then moved in together. Since we were pretty much inseparable from the start, we figured it was silly to pay two rents.

Brett and I both worked hard all week, but we let loose on the weekends. We'd go to a video arcade all day and then to a club to dance the night away. We made each other laugh, and Brett was the first man I felt completely and utterly comfortable with. We got married in 1996, a little less than two years after meeting. He was thirty-two and ready to settle down, and although I was only twenty, I was ready for marriage as well.

Sure, I was young, but I had always felt older than my biological age. I was raised by a single mom, which forced me to grow up faster than most, and I learned to fend for myself early on. If I wanted to get all Freudian I guess I could say that Brett came off like a father figure, wanting to care for me, but putting all that aside, he really and truly was my best friend. We were two peas in a pod, finishing each other's sentences and making up for each other's weaknesses.

Even after we married, we were like two puppy dogs in love. We were that annoying couple you always yell at to "Get a room!" Our lives were consumed with each other, our careers, and traveling the world. The only sticking point revolved around me being sick (a.k.a. female problems). Because of Brett's OI, he had spent much of his childhood in and out of hospitals. As an adult, he had a hard time dealing with anything concerning illness, doctors, and especially hospitals.

When I was sick, I naturally wanted, no *needed* his compassion to help me heal, but I knew what Brett had been through so I let him off fairly easily. I went through my surgeries alone and dealt with much of it by myself. Perhaps if I hadn't let him off so easily we wouldn't have had the problems we did later, but who could have known what was to come?

In 1998, we moved into our dream house. Our business was doing great, I was doing well in school, and we were planning our family. And you know the next part of the story. Our firstborn spent the next three years in and out of hospitals. This tested our marriage for sure.

When Abigail had those first few seizures, we were caught in a whirlwind from pediatrician's office to the neonatal intensive care unit in a matter of hours. People poked her everywhere to take blood out and put IVs in. We could hear her crying all the way down the hall, and Brett and I held each other for dear life.

From that first night in the hospital, we didn't leave each other's side. We were scared and depressed together, leaning on each other for support and comfort. We took turns eating, bathing, and sleeping, knowing without saying a word that neither of us wanted to leave Abi's side. Our marriage, our partnership, was flawless those first few weeks. Brett was on daddy autopilot, not thinking about anything except getting through things with his wife and little girl.

But when the hospital stays started multiplying and began to get longer and more drawn out, Brett was reminded of his numerous hospital stays as a child. Memories came flooding back to him of lying on a hospital bed in traction for weeks at a time over and over again. It began to get harder and harder for him, and soon he could no longer stay with us in the hospital around the clock.

While logically I knew that Brett simply didn't have the emotional capacity to be there with us twenty-four hours a day, I was angry at him for not just sucking it up and dealing with it. I was going through complete sleep deprivation, not to mention claustrophobia from sitting in a cramped hospital room day after day. Plus I was totally alone, removed from all my friends and family. I became bitter and distant, closing Brett out in order to deal with the situation. Of course that didn't make things better, and shortly after we got Abi's diagnosis, Brett and I sought counseling to heal the rift that had come between us.

In therapy I learned to talk about my feelings rather than point fingers and make accusations at Brett. The therapist showed us that we could drown ourselves in the negative, but what good would that do? Instead she gave us homework that taught us to be constructive and also focus on the positive. Each week she asked a different question that we'd have to explore later at home in our own minds and write out on a piece of paper. These were questions like "What would you like to change about your relationship?" and "What did you like best about each other when you first met compared to how you feel today?"

One of the most important issues we talked about with the therapist was how to deal with medical problems. We knew that Abigail would have a lifetime of them, and it was crucial that we find a compromise. After many hours of counseling, we decided that from then on, Brett would come to visit for short periods of time, which would let me know he cared, but not for so long that it caused him anxiety.

Brett also began to come to doctors' appointments with us, but when it became too difficult for him, we decided I would go with Abigail alone and call him afterwards with the details.

For a while things got better. The homework helped and the exercises we did in therapy left us feeling better to the point that we stopped going. Even so, it seemed that everywhere we turned, the universe was plotting against us. As if all the medical problems we had with Abi weren't enough to stress our marriage, the financial burdens were a surefire killer. A special needs child can cost up to $150,000 a year. While some cost more and others less, the financial stress is enormous.

Can you afford the extra premiums (many health insurers charge extra for pre-existing conditions) for private insurance? Can you afford the equipment or therapies that aren't covered by the insurance companies? There's the home healthcare, the pharmacy bills, the co-pays, and the deductibles. Even if you can't afford insurance, Medicaid will still have you pulling from your pocket with high co-pays and limited medication coverage. The Medicaid budget has been slashed again and again in Florida – two million just this year and two million last year, too.

I have met families who waited over a year for a wheelchair just to find out that Medicaid changed the doctor's orders and gave them something not practical for them. One family I know complained that the wheelchair was too big and not convenient to travel with since it took twenty minutes to fit it in the car.

For our part, we waited almost a year for a chair to bathe Abigail in – the one we had was eight years old and she'd outgrown it – but Medicaid denied the claim for some ridiculous reason I can't even explain (and neither could they, after six phone calls). I finally gave up and paid for the chair myself.

School costs can be high as well. Do you put the child in private school? Hire an advocate or lawyer? The special food adds up, as do the other medical supplies that aren't covered. The possible nursing care you need either today or tomorrow can add up, too. The financial demands alone are enough to pull a marriage apart, especially if you are like Brett and me, who wouldn't settle for anything less than the best doctors, equipment, and therapies for Abi. Before we had ripped off the last check in our checkbook for 2007, we realized we had spent well near that $150,000 that year on Abi's care.

Brett and I own our own business and make a good living, but it's a huge stressor to have to make enough to care for Abigail. Brett busts his butt doing sales and marketing, every week starting at zero, and it's not easy. When we first started I helped run the business with office management, human resources, and finances. Since we didn't have to pay someone to do that we could keep much of the profit ourselves, but as time went on I was able to do less and less. I went from working fifty-five hours a week before Abigail to just fifteen hours a week after she was born.

We had to re-evaluate the finances several times — what could we cut out? What couldn't we cut out? What could we push off? We slashed expensive dinners and any kind of upscale travel. We put off non-required maintenance on the house and made deals with our neighbors to help share the cost of required maintenance like cutting the grass and taking care of the pool. We added extra insulation to our house and office to cut electricity, added fans, and installed hot water timers. At the office we cut staff Christmas bonuses and asked our sales agents to supply their own office chairs and telephone headsets. We ran the business and household tight because we knew we couldn't take away from Abigail.

In addition to the day-to-day financial concerns, we also had to face the future. My biggest fear was, and remains, *Who will take care of our daughter if something happens to Brett and me, and how will they afford it?* Brett took all my fears, internalized them, and began to work like a dog to put savings away for Abigail's future. This added yet another stress to our marriage. He was working around the clock, while I was left to focus on Abigail's health and progress, not to mention my responsibilities around the house and with the business.

All in all, there was a great deal of stress on our marriage. It didn't matter whether we were busting our hump to pay today's bills or planning for the future; either way the stress was mounting and we found our relationship hurting again. The money coming in was never enough.

Since Brett is the money maker, he felt the world on his shoulders, and I think he often felt alone in this particular responsibility. Although I do help in the office, it was and essentially is his responsibility to make sure Abigail is taken care of financially for the rest of her life. He works long days, and he's always looking for ways to improve and better his sales. He comes home beat up and exhausted and he needs a break, not necessarily our crazy, physically demanding household. I am sure other dads feel that way too, but in our family, where the demands are higher than most, it's particularly complicated.

Brett used to work non-stop, talking and working through the evening while we were eating, playing, and longing for his attention. By the time he finally relaxed and turned work off, everyone was ready for bed – including me – which left little time for romance.

We finally went back into therapy and realized we needed to change our schedules to make time for the family, to make time for us as a couple, and to make time for us as individuals. We learned to literally schedule our time: 5:30 is now family dinner time and 8:30 is when couple time begins every night. We also make sure we have the occasional individual nights to ourselves to read, work, hang out with friends, or watch television. And we're constantly speaking to each other about how we are feeling that week – do we need more couple time or more individual time? Again, after years of being in and out of couples' therapy, we have a better handle on things but for years we missed each other.

Brett and I have a saying: "Life gets in the way of our love." As an adult you have several different responsibilities and they can take over if you let them, but you can't. The reality is that husbands and wives should come first. You are always going to need each other for emotional and financial support. Every marriage therapist we've ever been to has told us the same thing: put your spouse first and everything will fall into place. I had a hard time with this myself, always wanting to put the kids first, but the reality was the therapists were right.

We have made a lot of changes by setting some ground rules: no phones during dinner and at least thirty minutes of family time after dinner every night. We also have give and take: Brett lets me sleep in one day a week and I stay up late with him two nights a week. We also have date night at least one night a week, which helps us feel like husband and wife and not just mommy and daddy. We work together cooking, cleaning, and taking care of the kids, and we try to see what makes us happy as individuals as opposed to always making our kids happy. Together, we read a great book called *The Five Languages of Love* that talks about each person's "love tank" and how we fill our love tanks according to words, touch, action, and more.

While reading this book, Brett and I realized our loneliness had evolved into anger and hurt. Thanks to counseling and several additional books, we are now on a better road.

Over the years, we had been guilty of doing a lot of things wrong – communication was the biggest. For a time we pretty much shut each other out. We worked side by side but not together, and it was a vicious cycle – the more I shut him out, the more he worked, and the more he worked, the more I shut him out of my thoughts and feelings. We were living parallel lives with built-up hostility. It was explosive, and we finally hit bottom and began to swim up. Slowly we repaired the wounds. Every day we work at it, but the reality is that we are better together than apart. There are now more good days than bad, and we don't take each other for granted any more.

Over our twelve years of marriage, we've gone into counseling three different times. The last time, just this past year, things were the worst they've ever been. When a marriage is in trouble, it takes twice as much time and effort to fix it. If you don't put everything you have into it, you can sink.

I must admit, neither of us was putting the work into it that it needed. We nearly sank. We even filed for divorce. But we continued in therapy, and we finally came to the conclusion that we did still love each other for the same reasons we married in the first place. That love was hidden for a while, covered by the hurt we both felt, but we realized that if we made changes in our lifestyle to help decrease the stress, we would be better together than apart.

I realize today how important it is to have that third person, that mediator, to help a marriage along when times get tough. The odds have been against us with Abigail and the extra stress that comes with her. Our poor communication skills worked against us, too. Keeping the focus on us, as a couple, has been hard over the past several years, but today we realize that it's an essential key to a successful marriage.

9

The All-Essential
Support System

*T*here are times in our lives when we all need a helping hand to get things done, advice to help us through a stressful time, or maybe just a shoulder to cry on. The saying "It takes a village to raise a child" couldn't apply more to our special children. It may be hard to take care of a healthy child by yourself, but it is ten, one hundred, maybe even one thousand times harder to take care of a sick child by yourself. In fact, I'd venture to say it's impossible.

After all, our adorable children require an enormous amount of attention. Feeding a child a bowl of cereal, for instance, takes perhaps five minutes with a typical child. With Abi, it can take up to an hour. Dressing a typical child takes minutes, but dressing Abi takes twenty minutes from start to finish. Every single thing I do with Abi takes at least twice the amount of time – or longer – than it would with a typical child.

Nonetheless, it was not easy for me to admit I needed help. I fought it tooth and nail. I was raised in a big Italian family and my motherly role model was Grandma Carol, who raised six children on her own. No nannies, no baby nurses, no cleaning ladies, no takeout food. And believe me, my Italian grandfather was more like a seventh child than a helper and Grandma still managed to do things just fine.

Grandma Carol was born in 1927 in Newark, New Jersey, where she met my grandfather, Tom. They lived there until 1950 when they moved to Hialeah, Florida. By the time she was thirty-nine she had five children, and when she made the discovery that she was pregnant with number six, she was nervous. "How am I going to afford six children?" she asked her mother. "How will I manage it all?"

My great-grandmother told her daughter that these children are "the fruit of your love" and that Carol was blessed. From that moment on, Grandma Carol was at peace, raising her six children. She even worked outside the home, helping my grandfather in their hardware store and taking late-night phone calls for their locksmith services. Without a stitch of help, Grandma did it all. Those six children all got married and had their own children, I among them, and we all heard the stories of how Grandma did it all herself. Heck, she even did it before laundry machines and frozen dinners, so what was I doing complaining about raising one kid?

Like my grandmother, I thought I could do it all, all by myself. It was hard for me to admit I couldn't. But I finally realized after much angst that we all need help, even the strongest amongst us.

Let me go back to the beginning of my story a bit to explain. Soon after Abigail was born, when she started having problems, I pushed all my friends away. I just didn't have time for them. I was too busy running from doctor to doctor, hospital to hospital, problem after problem, and diagnosis after diagnosis. I didn't mean to push them all away; it just happened. Eventually, when I kept pushing, they retreated.

When Abigail was around six months old, I hit my breaking point. I was sitting on the couch and Brett asked me why I was so quiet. As you've probably realized by now, that's seldom the case with me.

I lost it. I cried and then cried some more. I looked at myself, unshowered and still dressed in pregnancy clothes. The house was a wreck, the mail was piled up, our finances were unbalanced. My life revolved around doctors' visits, medical procedures, and prescriptions. Everything that didn't represent me was everywhere I turned, and I was losing my grip on reality.

I had no control and no drive to do anything but exist, but as I sat there in my living room, I realized I felt like a stranger to myself. This wasn't *me*. I needed to take control of my happiness and my family's happiness. I took a deep breath and told Brett, "We can't do this by ourselves any more. We have no marriage, we have no fun, and we no longer exist as people." We talked all night, and together we realized we needed help. Thank goodness we got it, for it pulled us through the roughest times in our lives.

Since that day, I have honed my support system into four major areas: emotional support, pleasure support, schedule support, and us time support. These categories are not scientific; there's no research behind them or anything like that. They're from the Danielle Zimmerman School of Experience, created through my own internal evaluation of my life and realizing what I need in order to achieve some semblance of balance.

Make no mistake; all four systems are crucial. Without them, I would be living in a padded room weaving baskets (sometimes, I must admit, basket weaving has its benefits). I hope that by sharing my personal support systems, you'll put some in place for yourself. Trust me, you, your husband, and your kids will be happier.

Analyze your life to see if you have one, some, or all of these support systems already in place. I'll bet you've got some. If so, hold on to them for dear life. If not, you've got to add some. Believe me, they will save you.

Let me explain further. Have you ever noticed that when you're feeling really low, a simple conversation can make you feel a whole lot better? If this has happened to you, you've already experienced the benefit of my first type of support system, the emotional support system.

Everyone needs people around them to whom they can speak freely about their thoughts and feelings. Perhaps a friend, parent, spouse, sister-in-law, maybe all of the above. Psychotherapists can also be wonderful additions to the emotional support system. After all, your plate is so big, you'll need several people to pull this off. There's no shame in seeing a therapist. I've been there, done that, gotten the t-shirt, and it's a wonderful thing.

The fact is, different people serve different emotional needs. My husband, for example, wants to solve my problems. This isn't unusual, since men seem to have a biological need to solve everything. Other people in my life offer an ear, whether or not they understand what I'm going through, and whether or not they can offer any solutions.

My mom is particularly good at providing sympathy. I remember her once telling me that I rarely look at her as a daughter seeking answers from a mother but rather as a friend seeking an ear from another friend. I am thankful my relationship with my mother allows me that. I know not everyone has that luxury.

For a long time I thought I didn't have time to spend with friends – breakfast, coffee, or even a quick phone call took too much time away from Abi. But now that I realize how important my emotional support system is, now that I know I couldn't do my job as a mother half as well without it, I make that time. Sometimes I force that time. I carve it out of my schedule and make sure I don't miss it. Occasionally, I admit, I only manage one hushed, late-night phone call during the week. Other weeks I share a twenty-minute cup of coffee with a group of friends. Somehow, someway, I fit it in.

Recently, I found a great emotional release with Brett by reading together. A classic book we love to read aloud is Paul Reiser's *Couplehood*. It makes us laugh at each other's habits and it also gives us an opportunity to talk about our feelings in a light, humorous way.

The second system I rely on is what I call the pleasure support system. This is basically the ability to enjoy your family without the daily strains of work, housework, bills, homework, and therapy appointments. The pleasure support system is just that –pleasures. Entertainment, fun, joy. You can join other couples or families for outings, fairs, concerts, dinners, vacations – the normal things families do together. That good wholesome fun can energize you and help you cope with everything you're dealing with. I find at those times that I don't worry about the medical problems, the therapy goals, the bills, or the cleaning. Our family just lets loose, enjoys the moment, and revels in each other.

One of our favorite and most simple pleasures is going to the movies. I bring a beach bag filled with items that will keep Abigail comfortable and occupied like pillows and a blanket, a chewy necklace, and other non-noisy toys. (After all, we don't want to disturb the other moviegoers!) Although Abi may not necessarily understand the entire movie, going to the theater is a treat for her too. She has no demands to exercise, communicate properly, or act appropriately. She loves that she can just relax and do what she enjoys most – chew on non-edible objects and watch a movie.

Of course I don't usually let Abigail sit and chew on necklaces, but for those two hours I let her relax and enjoy herself so that I can relax and enjoy myself. My mother always told me to choose my battles. Well, when it comes to simple pleasure time, there are no battles. We all get to sit back, relax, and savor the moment.

"Simple pleasures" is a bit of a misnomer, because some pleasures are not so simple. They require planning and more support. For example, we always take at least a few family vacations a year. Sure, they can be challenging, but with a little preparation and a lot (ahem) of organization, the challenge is absolutely worth it. I always spend one full day before we leave organizing. I start by making a list of things I need to buy, need to pack, and need to grab as we walk out the door. If we're driving, we take hiking backpacks rather than diaper bags since we can fit more in them and they have handy organizational compartments. When we fly, sometimes I actually buy certain items at our destination rather than lug them on the plane with us. Things like Pediasure, diapers, wipes, water, and other necessities are available at any local drug or grocery store, so instead of packing them all up, I just pick them up locally. A few times I've actually mailed our belongings to the hotel because I've found that the price of shipping is worth the cost of saving my sanity. (Isn't your sanity worth something?)

I always call ahead to make sure every place we'll be going is accessible for wheelchairs. Once we arrive, I spend about two hours each morning planning for the rest of the day. I type a daily agenda so my husband and I know exactly where we're going that day and who needs to do what in order to reach our destination safely and happily.

I always make sure to plan breakfast, lunch, and dinner because I know my husband won't think ahead. (I know all you women reading this are nodding your heads!) Like most things with Abi, mealtimes require planning. Even our typical son gets extremely cranky and incoherent if we wait too long to feed him, so planning is essential. If I can strategize in the morning, I can enjoy myself for the rest of the day. You may call me a control freak, but I would rather control the situation than have it control me.

Sure, family outings and vacations can be tougher with a special needs child. That's why we always invite family, friends, or a babysitter to come along and lend a hand (or two). When you go away, don't be afraid to ask others to come with you, and give everyone a job or responsibility.

My husband and I know that we cannot travel any longer without help. Experience has taught us that when we do so, our bodies ache and we crave sleep more than when we left. When you're physically and mentally drained, it's no vacation. If you don't have someone to help, see if you can get a nurse or respite care provided by Medicaid. Whether it's for two hours, two days, or two weeks, everyone needs a break once in a while.

Developing the next category, the schedule support system, was the hardest for me. As I've said before, I was raised in a big Italian family and was taught how to care for a family in old-Italian fashion – i.e., mothers do everything. But now I realize that here in the twenty-first century, truly good multi-tasking requires help from experts. Teachers, coaches, spouses, friends, and neighbors are all there for a reason: to help you make it through your week. If everyone helps add a little sanity to your life, you won't have the opportunity to go insane trying to do everything yourself.

I include the school system in the schedule support system as well. Being able to drop your child off, knowing he or she is in good hands while you have a few hours to yourself, is a great comfort, though it might take eliminating a few schools to find the right one.

As you know, we home schooled Abi before opening Abi's Place, but it is still the same basic idea. We had a wonderful teacher and several therapists who came to our home to give Abigail what she needed and deserved. Our health insurance also allowed us to have additional speech, physical, and occupational therapists. Because I had such faith and confidence in them, I didn't have to hover and watch their every move. They gave us advice when it was needed, helped us with Abigail's daily living skills, and gave me the occasional moment to reconcile the bank account, answer emails, and go to the bathroom by myself!

I can't leave my husband out of the weekly schedule support system. As time has gone by, he's learned to step up to the plate more than I ever dreamed possible. Today Brett is a huge support, helping me with cooking, cleaning, bathing, and laundry. We tag team mornings and nights with the kids, house chores, grocery shopping, and work.

Finally, the last category is the "us time" support system. This allows time for my husband and me to get away from the kids to relax and rejuvenate. It's time for husband and wife. Danielle can finally see herself as an individual person who can be sexy, an intellectual, and viewed without kids hanging around her hip, and Brett can do the same. This is the support system that can re-kindle your marriage. It can allow you to be who you were before you had kids.

Some of your "us" time can actually be done alone, playing golf, getting a massage, or even treating yourself to a pedicure. I try to get to go to the gym twice a week, but I'm satisfied when I make it there at least once. I know I have a crazy schedule and I'm a realist. Brett watches the kids for those forty-five minutes and I'm able to burn off some energy and get some stress relief, knowing he's spending quality time with them.

By the way, I definitely notice a difference if I don't get to the gym. After about two weeks I feel myself getting depressed, so I really make the effort.

My husband's favorite thing to do during his "us time" is take a nap. I admit I used to get mad when he napped. *What a waste of time*, I thought. But then I realized this is just his preferred way to spend his free time, and he's as entitled as I am to do what he likes.

Other "us" time is for both of us, like going on a weekend (or longer) vacation without the kids. In addition, my husband and I have date night once a week. It's not easy to do all the time – we're tired, we don't want to spend the money on a babysitter – but we literally force ourselves, because we know how important it is. To save money, we have family and friends babysit as often as they can. Just recently, we started a barter system with friends. One weekend we watch their kids and the next they watch ours. Although they have two typical children and aren't used to Abigail's special needs, we give her all her medicines and put her to bed before we go out.

I'll let you in on a little secret. Over the years, Brett and I have developed a mutual hobby we enjoy during our "us time." Don't laugh – it's poker! Growing up in my family, we always played some type of cards. As a teenager, I played Spades religiously. Brett was also a big card player while growing up, and when the two of us first met, we realized this was a mutual interest. We enjoyed it so much that we actually flew to the Bahamas to play blackjack several times before having kids. Soon, poker began to catch on as a popular sport, so we naturally gravitated toward it.

We wanted to do it right, so we studied the game in and out and began playing two times a week at the local Indian casinos. We even began traveling to play, and before we knew it, we were disciplined and serious about our playing.

Now I use poker as a stress reliever. It gives me an opportunity to be just an average Jill Schmoe rather than the mom of a child with special needs or a business owner, just a girl who likes to play cards. It gives me some normalcy.

Don't get me wrong. It's not that we ever disown the fact that our daughter is Abigail. But really, at the poker table, no one has the identity of mother, father, doctor, lawyer, or policeman…We're all just poker players. Brett and I need that since our lives are otherwise consumed with taking care of Abigail.

I know my breakdown of support systems isn't scientific or fancy, but it makes sense. I have talked to many parents over the years whose children have special needs, and plenty of parents of typical children who feel overwhelmed. For all of us, whether it's someone to listen to you complain about your husband over a cup of coffee, a therapist who teaches your child how to kick a ball, or a group of friends who understand that your life is different than theirs and start the dinner party early to accommodate your daughter's medicine schedule, everyone needs help. Me included.

10

The Roller Coaster
of Emotions

Here I am, pouring my heart out to you and getting more personal than I have with anyone in my entire life, so it seems only natural to discuss the emotional roller coaster I have been on with Abigail for the past ten years (Ten years? Can Abigail really be ten now? It's hard to believe…) I have experienced a great many ups and downs during this time, and I'd like to share a few lessons I've learned along the way.

As parents of special needs children, we tend to oscillate between the dark and the sunny side. In other words, we tend to think, and often dwell, on the fact that life has handed us the worst possible thing imaginable. Woe is me. This is awful. Why did this have to happen to us? Everything looks bleak and ugly.

Suddenly we flip to moments of joy and happiness. Innocent laughter or a sly smile can put things in perspective. When you reach a milestone, whether it's your daughter walking at age three or your son saying his first word at six months, you celebrate with laughter and tears, running to the phone to share the news with relatives and friends. You revel in the success for both of you…the hard work your child has put in and the hard work you have put in making sure she never gives up.

But then the dark side sets in again, after the kids have gone to bed and you're alone in your thoughts. She is five and walking with a walker. She's seven and still can't communicate verbally. Why? Why does this have to be so hard? You ask "Why?" again and again. You feel your child's pain, witness the months and years of hard work that don't always pay off. You can't help asking yourself why it has to be this way.

I feel your pain, friends. I've been through it all myself. The ride that goes up must come down. Isn't that the law of physics? (Is it really physics or just a top forty hit?) Wherever the saying comes from, there are inevitably going to be downs in life, but over the years I have learned not to get stuck in the downs. I enjoy the ups, weather the downs, and keep on climbing back up. Sometimes it takes some doing to get out of the hole, but I promise, it can be done. You may be in the depths of depression right this minute, but don't wallow in it. Push as hard as you can to get out. If you're deep in the depths, it is my fervent hope that you'll feel better by the end of this chapter.

Of course, I am not totally out in la-la land. I too have ridden the roller coaster and gotten stuck at the bottom. It's taken years for me to get to where I am today. From the very start of our journey, when we first found out we were pregnant, I was elated but also hesitant because of Brett's family history of OI. But when we found out I was carrying a girl, the hesitation disappeared since we thought (incorrectly as it turns out) that OI only affects boys.

The day Abigail was born, I cried tears of joy, cradling our little girl and staring at her with pure love. Brett sat on the bed too with a twinkle in his eye, amazed by the beauty of his wife and baby girl. He was beyond joy because he had a little girl who didn't suffer from his genetic bone disorder.

Then, as quickly as our joy appeared, it vanished. Our world was crushed when Abi's seizures began. Ten long days in that first hospital and two and a half weeks in the second was a roller coaster of tests and procedures, and my emotions followed suit. Abigail couldn't regulate her own temperature. We weren't allowed to take her out of the incubator because it was too dangerous. Her temperature could drop too rapidly, which would cause more seizures and ultimately stop her breathing.

I was hit pretty hard when the nurses sent me out of the NICU because they needed a sterile environment for the invasive procedures they were about to perform. They poked Abi like a voodoo doll while she cried in pain and all I could do was stand helplessly by the door, peeking through the window. I felt like my world was spinning out of control.

I couldn't comfort my daughter, I couldn't fix her problems, I couldn't take her away from it all, and my maternal instinct was telling me to do all of the above. Rendered completely helpless, I felt like someone was literally ripping my heart out.

But I refused to break down. My only choice – no, the only thing I knew how to do – was go into survival mode. Despite feeling like I couldn't breathe and wasn't even sure if I could make it through the day, I made sure to eat and drink so I could pump enough breast milk to nourish Abi. That was what I could do to take care of her. Finally, when they were finished with the IVs, the blood drawings, the spinal taps, and all the other tests and procedures, we held on to Abi like our lives depended on it. I guess in a way they did.

Then the uncertainty nearly killed me. Had the seizures caused brain damage? Was she going to stop breathing? Was she going to live through the night? When my mind wandered into those dark places, I did my best to stuff such questions deep into my soul because I just couldn't bear the thought of losing our daughter. At one point, we did call the priest in to bless her because we thought she might not make it, but even then I didn't actually feel I was going to lose her. At that time, denial was the only way I could deal with the situation.

This denial, I believe, was the first stage of grief for me. I talked about the five stages of grief earlier: denial and isolation, anger, bargaining, depression, and acceptance. In the initial days of Abigail's illness, I was going through the first stage. While Abigail was still alive, the grief I experienced was for the daughter I had lost – the daughter with whom I was going to get my nails done and with whom I was going to laugh and joke and go shopping and watch walk down the aisle one day. Now, because of everything that was happening, I wasn't sure if any of that was going to happen. So I stuffed my grief down below the surface and denied, denied, denied.

Soon enough, those feelings morphed into anger, which I turned on my ob/gyn. I was furious at him for denying me the amnio in the first place, for not alerting me about how small Abi was when she was born, for writing down her small head circumference but never diagnosing anything or telling me about all the problems it could lead to.

By the time we got to Miami Children's Hospital, I had reached the bargaining phase. I promised God I would be the best mother possible. Brett and I would give our daughter the best doctors, the best hospitals, and work as many jobs as needed to pay for them. We would do everything within our means and beyond to make Abi better. We wanted her to live. We wanted the seizures to end. We wanted a diagnosis.

And then, when we got what we wanted – a diagnosis – I hit depression. This was the one and only time I became completely and utterly out of control. Microcephaly. I did my computer research and there it was in black and white: short life expectancy. The reasoning ability of a monkey. Oh my God…Our sweet, precious girl might not live past her teenage years.

I felt absolutely helpless and the tears just rolled down my face. Despair set in and I cried until there were no tears left. The dishes piled up, the laundry was strewn throughout the house, and I could hardly get off the couch. I stood by the kitchen sink and cried my eyes out. Exhausted, I realized I needed help. I just couldn't handle the wallowing anymore. While there's some comfort in wallowing, I knew it wasn't helping me, it wasn't helping Brett, and it certainly wasn't helping Abi.

I began to see a psychotherapist. She stressed to me how important it was that I not lose myself in Abi's diagnosis. I had to take care of my daughter, but I also had to take care of myself.

This was a completely foreign concept to me. As I explained in the last chapter, my mother and grandmother never put their needs in the equation, let alone put them first. "Give, give, give" was their motto. As I mentioned earlier, I was raised by a single mother who worked three jobs to make sure my brother, sister, and I had a roof over our heads and food to eat. We had only the bare essentials but we always had fun making the best of it. As my mother reminded me just last week, she is still amazed how she pulled it off living on thirty-five dollars a week for groceries for four of us. I remember my mom won some money in a contest when we were little and rather than going shopping and buying some badly needed items for herself, she took us kids to Disney World for the first time. Around Christmas time, my wonderful mother would dress up as Miss Claus and pump gas. Well, I won't go into great detail about that one even though it was on roller skates. She wanted to help bring the holiday spirit to others…all for free. Perhaps it is just a motherly thing. You naturally want to do for others rather than for yourself.

But in talking to the therapist, I realized that if I didn't take care of myself, I wouldn't be able to take care of Abi. She convinced me to think about myself and what I needed. The first thing that came to mind was my education. It had taken a backseat when Abigail was born. Since I loved learning, I registered for some online classes.

Miraculously, I was invigorated again. The first few weeks of class registration, getting my books, starting the classes – it all fed on itself. Sure, I had to force myself to begin, but as soon as I did, I felt like a new person and was propelled through the next step. It was exactly what I needed to get back to myself, back to the person who could best help Abigail.

Little by little, I reached acceptance. Acceptance that I couldn't change Abi but that I could do my best to help her. In order to do that, I couldn't get trapped in the downside of the roller coaster. In the simplest terms, I decided that I just wasn't going to go to the dark side again.

This is hard, and sometimes it's almost impossible. I confess I've had my setbacks. Only a few months after I made my decision not to go to the dark side, I plummeted back down anyway. Abi was around seven or eight months old and the MRI showed she had brain atrophy. I plunged down that roller coaster, picturing portions of Abi's brain just dying. I imagined her as a vegetable, and all I could do was lie in bed and stare at the ceiling while the tears rolled down my face. All of it hurt so bad; my heart just ached with love and disappointment. Why was this happening? What had I done wrong?

I couldn't help feeling somehow responsible, even though I knew I hadn't caused Abi's problems. I hadn't drunk when I was pregnant, I hadn't done drugs, I hadn't smoked. I'd never shaken her as an infant, even when she was crying all night. I couldn't help asking God, asking whomever, "What did I do to deserve this? What did Abigail do? She's just a baby – what could she possibly have done to deserve all the pain she's suffered?"

But it's like the old saying about seeing the glass half full or half empty. For the most part, I try to see it as half full. This is our reality, and I have been given this child for a reason, for better or worse, through sickness and health. It's a commitment. We take wedding vows to show commitment to our spouses, so why not our children, too? Isn't that the meaning of unconditional love, loving them no matter what? For this reason, I have tried my best over the years to see the sunny side of things, no matter how deep that sunny side is buried.

Let me see if I can explain a little better. A perfect example is when we were in Baltimore and Abigail was in restraints 24/7. It was hard to see her like that, but I knew the restraints were better than her beating herself up, and I was hopeful the restraints would one day no longer be necessary. I was able to rationalize what we were doing.

She was safe with the restraints on. She wasn't abusing herself, and that overshadowed the awfulness of the restraints.

Just the other day I was looking at pictures and I found one from a trip to the zoo we took during that time. In the picture, she's wearing the restraints. Now, looking at it, I think, "Oh my gosh, that looks horrible!" But I can think back to where I was then, knowing this was an important step on the road to getting better.

It was the same for the multiple hospital stays. I hated when Abi was in the hospital, both for her and for me. For weeks at a time I had to live in a tiny room, stripped of the comforts of home. It felt like a jail cell, but I resigned myself to it because that's what Abi needed to get better and I had to do what was best for her. Sure, I could have slumped into depression, but what good would that have done Abi? I had to put on a happy face and go through the motions because I knew this was going to help her in the end.

Brett had an even tougher time with it all than I did. I think in general men and women behave very differently when it comes to the emotions involved in dealing with their children. Mothers tend to take it all on themselves. They immerse themselves in the child, losing themselves completely in them. Fathers tend to bury themselves in their work, using it as a coping mechanism, or they run away from it altogether.

Brett was amazing during Abi's first stay in the hospital, but after that, he ran away. He didn't come to any of her tests or attempt to find out the results, and as I've said to you in previous chapters, that didn't sit well with me. When we were in Kennedy Krieger, Brett couldn't stand to see Abi hit herself and he literally ran away – he flew back home and told me he'd see us when we were finished. I was furious with him, and believe me, there have been plenty of times since then when I've been furious with him.

I've steadied our relationship's roller coaster by realizing that Brett and I are two very different people and the way we cope with things is therefore very different. Nonetheless, it's taken years, plus many hours of therapy, to come to that realization.

When Ethan was born, our lives took a whole new turn on the roller coaster. As happy as we were to have a typical child, it was also a bit sad. Ethan is a daily reminder of all the things Abigail will never be. But, in Danielle fashion, I flip the coin and remind myself that Abigail is so much better *because* of Ethan.

He's the one who taught her to crawl, he's the one who motivated her to walk, he's the one who motivated her to eat real food. She worked and worked at it, and now she's eating everything we eat. Remember, I'm Italian, which means my daughter can pack in some chicken parmesan.

Before Abi was vocalizing at all, Ethan made noises that fascinated her and suddenly she was making noises too. She idolized every little thing he did, and she still does. To watch her light up when he kisses her makes my heart sing. So while you can say it's bittersweet to watch him grow and flourish while she has trouble with everything, I choose to focus on the fact that *because* of all the ways he flourishes, she prospers as well.

Would you like to know another glass half full opportunity? People staring at us in public. I know some parents of special needs kids get annoyed, frustrated, or embarrassed by it. A mom told me just the other day that she just wants to tell people staring at her child to "F-off."

I take a different approach. I actually welcome the stares, because I see them as opportunities to educate people. When I catch someone eyeing us, I introduce myself and ask if they have any questions. This often leads to a discussion that allows me to teach somebody about Abigail's disability. To be honest, I find such opportunities thrilling. For so many years people hid their special needs children in institutions, and some people still hide them in the house, which I think is heartbreaking.

I look at the stares from the other side. Let them stare, because that's how they're going to learn. People are usually staring for one overriding reason – because they're curious. I utilize that curiosity to my advantage, and these days Abi and I make friends wherever we go.

It's not always easy to turn your emotions on a dime like that. It's not always easy to see the sunny side, but it's really important to realize that while you can't change the world, you can change your perceptions of it.

One of the most important ways to change your perceptions is to take care of yourself. If I teach you one thing in this chapter, please resolve to take time for yourself. Take time to regroup and get yourself together so that you can handle the emotions that come your way. If you can't afford a babysitter to watch the kids while you head to the gym for an hour, wake up twenty minutes early and grab a cup of coffee and read the paper by yourself. Last night I stayed up for an extra hour and waxed myself. It was the highlight of my day! That may sound pathetic, but if you can find the time and energy to do something for yourself, to find the *you* in your life, you'll be able to steer the roller coaster up instead of down all the time.

Consider joining a support group. See if there's a special education PTA in your town, an internet support group, or some type of group run by your local hospital or a state agency. Often when I'm feeling down, I call up the scientist in me. I try to look at all the different angles and make sense of it all. No matter what I'm looking at, there's always a good side, a way to look at things to make it all seem not so bad. While you might say I'm in denial as to how grim our situation is, I counter with this: I accept the fact that my daughter has special needs and will never be able to live on her own. She may never walk without assistance. She may never eat without assistance. She may never read or run up a slide or fall in love.

But why dwell on that? Why not look at the good side of all those things? She may never walk up a slide, but I'll never be at the park worrying that she's going to break her leg. She may not fall in love, but I'll never have to worry about teen pregnancy, either. She will never truly be alone, but she'll never become a drug addict, and I'll never have to stay up nights worrying about where she is or who she's with or if she's safe.

The other day a mom called me whose child had just received a diagnosis of Angelman Syndrome. She was beside herself. "Why does my child have to suffer like this?" she asked me again and again. But one of the characteristics of Angelman Syndrome is a happy child who laughs excessively. "Your child won't suffer," I told her. "It's going to be a different life than you expected, but take comfort in the fact that your child will always be laughing."

I know this might sound crazy, but I truly feel that Abigail's issues are a blessing in disguise. No matter what is going on around her, she will always remain innocent and happy. She has come a long way and continues to make progress. We are at a different place today. Before our focus was keeping Abigail alive, finding medical answers, and getting her strong. Today we are focusing on developing her cognitive brain function and independence with limited assistance.

We are very proud of Abigail and all her hard work, which will continue every day she lives. She understands just about anything we say to her today. We use simple language of course, not crossword puzzle vocabulary. Thank God, since I don't know half those words myself. She is able to communicate with us using a combination of vocal sounds, gestures, sign language, and pictures. The world is a big amusement park and she wants to explore everything. She is curious about how the ketchup bottle works and also the cheese grater. I love watching her amazement when she discovers new little gizmos, like the lock box in the doctor's office she explored until she figured it out. When we got a new van she had to check out every feature, just like any other child. Through Abi, I get to be a kid and revel in the pure innocence life has to offer.

When you look at the world, in the scheme of it all, Abigail is better off than many kids, and I'm better off than many parents.

How Far
We've Come

*T*oday, Abigail is a blossoming ten-year-old girl who loves to play dress up, loves to go outside, and loves to ride roller coasters. The smile that delighted us all as a baby still lights up any room, and these days she has plenty to smile about. She, and we her parents, have come a long way since that horrible day in Dr. Bedside Manner's office.

When he told us she would have "the mental capacity of a monkey, with no reasoning or logical thinking," we weren't sure we were going to make it through the next day, let alone the next ten years, but Abigail has made incredible strides.

I remember how we had to teach her how to play with toys, step by step. We had to help her figure everything out: how does this toy work? What do you do? Do you shake it? Bounce it? Throw it? Push it? Push buttons? Now, not only does she know how to play with the toy herself, she can crawl over to her toy box, rummage through it to find the one she likes, and pull it out of the box herself. She no longer listens to Elmo over and over. She listens to Chris Brown and Katy Perry, as much as it annoys me.

For Christmas last year, Santa brought her a dancing light-up iDog to go with her iPod, and she loves to dance along with it. And, if you can believe it, we got her an EZ-Bake oven. She loves to bake things – the excitement mounts as she mixes and pours, and then of course, does some taste testing before it goes in the oven. After it's cooked, she's in heaven! Sure, we have to give her some physical assistance, but she understands what she needs to do. Mental capacity of a monkey, my ass.

Speaking of giving her physical assistance, she still walks with a walker, but she can also walk without it, just holding on to my hand. There are no more black and blue marks on her face from self-injurious behaviors. Every year since Abi and I returned from Kennedy Krieger, these behaviors have become less and less severe. Today we know exactly how to deal with them and so does the staff at school. Hurray!

I look back at those pictures, those days when she had to be restrained twenty-four hours a day, and I thank God we are not there anymore. A once frustrated little girl who didn't know how to get her point across now uses both hands appropriately, talks, points, picks up every item in sight, and gives hugs. The relief is amazing and the peace of mind, priceless. The future is stretched out right in front of us, and it's not scary anymore. When I think back to those days on the computer, reading about kids with microcephaly, I remember how terrified I was. Today, I don't think about the kids who die at a young age. Instead, I focus on the parents who have forty-year-old children living with microcephaly.

Of course, I understand that Abi probably won't ever leave home, have a job, or marry, but our family has quality of life now. We have a schedule and consistency, just like any other family, and I'm able to work just like any other twenty-first century mom, which I enjoy immensely.

Last year Abi began vocalizing, and today she makes about twenty different sounds, each with its own distinctive meaning. She has the "B" sound down really well, so she can indicate book, bubble, and basket. She also has the "C" sound so she can let me know when she wants to play with a toy car. Through fun, repetitious learning she picks up something new every day.

We introduced whistles to help with oral motor exercises and to help her push air out and suck it in, which you need to do in order to talk. After about a month of continuously working on it, she made noise with a tiny plastic whistle. Today, she plays the harmonica! She loves to B-box and she gives kisses with a real pucker with sound effects and all. She also signs a great deal to let us know what she wants. She's up to about fifty signs now and I don't see any hint of that stopping.

The girl who wouldn't let anything get close to her mouth now loves taking showers. I even bought her a hand-held sprayer because she loves the feeling of water hitting her mouth and body. She also loves to eat. In fact, she eats more different types of food than Ethan, my typical child. While she still has the feeding tube – and probably always will, due to all the medications she's on to prevent seizures and to help with her GI problems – she eats almost everything I cook. Chicken pot pie, sausage and gravy, eggs…You name it, she eats it. Though I have to puree much of what she eats, she can eat some things in their regular form like Cheerios, pizza, and even Pop Tarts. Now that the medication keeps her GI system under control, she's able to enjoy food.

In its first year, Abi's Place, also known as The Zimmerman School House, is exceeding every goal I had for it. We opened with four students and we're going to finish off the year with eight. We have one little girl who was basically kicked out of her school system. They had no place for her, they said, so how could I say no? Her county school system may have given up on her, but I sure as hell am not going to.

Since we started the school, every child has progressed, and Abi is no exception. In addition to all the academics she's being taught, she's learning patience. Remember, for her entire life, she's had dozens of people surrounding her and tending to her every need. At school, she's one of four in a classroom, so she has to share the attention. It's hilarious to watch. She folds her little hands on the desk and waits her turn. She also socializes with the other children, something she never had the opportunity to do before. I'm so proud of her. She's also learned to eat faster at school. At home she could basically sit at the kitchen table all day if she wanted to, but at school she only has a thirty- to forty-five-minute lunch period.

I can't begin to tell you what the school means to me. The dream that started with the birth of our beautiful daughter Abigail has now evolved into something bigger. It is no longer about one child but about many. Our little school will touch many needy lives. Although it's essential to our little girl, Abi's Place won't be just about one little girl's bright future, but about the bright futures of many in our community. It's a new beginning. Again. And this time we're ready for it.

Resource Guide

Websites

Many websites provide helpful information or sell products for special needs kids. Some of my favorite sites include the following:

www.sensoryresources.com

www.adaptivemall.com

www.abilitations.com

www.theraproducts.com

www.specialkidszone.com

www.adaptivechild.com

www.rifton.com (this website provides great seating options in a classroom or at home) *www.snugseat.com* (this website provides great mobility options in and out of the classroom)

www.therapyshoppe.com (this is where I find oral motor necklaces or rubbery materials with which to make necklaces)

www.hiphelpers.com (this site offers shorts that help lessen excessive hip abduction in babies and toddlers with low muscle tone)

www.behavioranalysts.com

www.monicadyerphotography.com (a photographer who specializes in working with special needs children)

Books and Magazines

The Out of Sync Child by Carol Stock Kranowitz

The Child with Special Needs by Stanley Greenspan

Teaching Language to Children with Autism or Other Developmental Disabilities (as known as ABLLS, a curriculum and overview on how to teach your child language using ABA techniques)

The Joys of Signing by Lottie Riekehof

Tools for Transition in Early Childhood by Beth S. Rous, Ed.D., and Rena A. Hallam, Ph.D.

Learn to Move, Move to Learn: Sensorimotor Early Childhood Activity Themes by Jenny Clark Brack

Playing, Laughing, and Learning with Children on the Autism Spectrum by Julia Moor (Though the book has autism in the title, it could be easily applied to any developmental disorder)

S.I. Focus, the international magazine dedicated to improving sensory integration (access it on the web at *www.sifocus.com*)

Advocacy

Log on to *www.wrightslaw.com* to learn more about your educational rights.

Log on to *http://idea.ed.gov*, part of the U.S. Department of Education's website, for an explanation of the Individuals with Disabilities Education Act.

Support Groups

Visit *www.disaboom.com*, a web community for people and families with special needs.

You can also join support groups at your local school as well as Easter Seals, Achievement Rehabilitation Center (ARC), or websites specific to your diagnosis such as Chromosome Disorder Outreach (*www.chromodisorder.org/CDO/*), United Cerebral Palsy (*www.ucp.org*), Autism Speaks (*www.autismspeaks.org*), and the National Association for Down Syndrome (*www.nads.org*).

Other

Deborah Dimare, a designer specializing in decorating to fit the sensory needs of children and adults, can be reached at *www. dimaredesign.com*.

Visit *www.healthgrades.com* to check out doctors' credentials and any legal action taken against individual doctors.

Visit *www.lifeorganizers.com* for great tips on time management in every aspect of life...home, work, travel, and kids.

Your local Children and Families Department in your area can also provide additional help.

Visit *www.abisplace.com*, our website, for further contact information.

Developmental Milestones for Babies

Reprinted with permission from March of Dimes

During the first year of life, your baby will grow and develop at an amazing speed. Her weight will double by five to six months and triple by her first birthday. And she is constantly learning. Major achievements, called developmental milestones, include rolling over, sitting up, standing, and possibly walking. And your heart will likely melt at the sound of her first "Mama" or "Dada."

However, no two babies are exactly alike. Your baby will develop at her own pace. Most babies reach certain milestones at similar ages. However, it's not unusual for a healthy "normal" baby to fall behind in some areas or race ahead in others.

The following milestones are only guidelines. Your baby's health care provider will evaluate your baby's development at each well-baby visit. Remember: always talk to your child's health care professional if you think your baby is lagging behind.

If your baby was born prematurely (before thirty-seven weeks of pregnancy), you need to look at the milestone guidelines a little differently. The age at which your baby is expected to reach various milestones is based on her due date, not her birthday. So if your baby was born two months early, she will most likely achieve milestones two months later than the guidelines below predict.

By the end of their first month, most babies:
- Make jerky, quivering arm movements
- Bring hands near face
- Keep hands in tight fists
- Move head from side to side while lying on stomach
- Focus on objects eight to twelve inches away
- Prefer human faces over other shapes
- Prefer black-and-white or high-contrast patterns
- Hear very well
- Recognize some sounds, including parents' voices

By the end of their third month, most babies:
- Raise head and chest when lying on stomach
- Support upper body with arms when lying on stomach
- Stretch legs out and kick when lying on stomach or back
- Push down on legs when feet are placed on a firm surface
- Open and shut hands
- Bring hands to mouth
- Grab and shake hand toys
- Follow moving object with eyes
- Watch faces closely
- Recognize familiar objects and people at a distance
- Start using hands and eyes in coordination
- Begin to babble and to imitate some sounds
- Smile at the sound of parents' voices
- Enjoy playing with other people
- May cry when playing stops

By the end of their seventh month, most babies:

- Roll over both ways (stomach to back and back to stomach)
- Sit up
- Reach for object with hand
- Transfer objects from one hand to the other
- Support whole weight on legs when held upright
- Develop full-color vision and mature distance vision
- Use voice to express joy and displeasure
- Respond to own name
- Babble chains of consonants (ba-ba-ba-ba)
- Distinguish emotions by tone of voice
- Explore objects with hands and mouth
- Struggle to get objects that are out of reach
- Enjoy playing peek-a-boo
- Show an interest in mirror images

By their first birthday, most babies:

- Sit without assistance
- Get into hands-and-knees position
- Crawl
- Pull self up to stand
- Walk holding onto furniture, and possibly a few steps without support
- Use pincer grasp (thumb and forefinger)
- Say "Dada" and "Mama"
- Use exclamations such as "Oh-oh!"
- Try to imitate words
- Respond to "No" and simple verbal requests
- Use simple gestures, such as shaking head "No" and waving bye-bye
- Explore objects in many ways (shaking, banging, throwing, dropping)
- Begin to use objects correctly (drinking from cup, brushing hair)

- Find hidden objects easily
- Look at correct picture when an image is named

By their second birthday, most children:
- Walk alone
- Pull toys behind them while walking
- Carry large toy or several toys while walking
- Begin to run
- Kick a ball
- Climb on and off furniture without help
- Walk up and down stairs while holding on to support
- Scribble with crayon
- Build tower of four blocks or more
- Recognize names of familiar people, objects, and body parts
- Say several single words (by fifteen to eighteen months)
- Use simple phrases (by eighteen to twenty-four months)
- Use two- to four-word sentences ("Want snack")
- Follow simple instructions
- Begin to sort objects by shapes and colors
- Begin to play make-believe
- Imitate behavior of others
- Show growing independence

Source: American Academy of Pediatrics. *Caring for Your Baby and Young Child: Birth to Age 5, Fourth Edition* (Bantam Books, 2005)

Abigal's Schedule

revised Aug. 23, 2008   calories 1100

8:00	**Prevacid** Dissolve 30mg tablet in 10 cc of water	**Reglan** 3.0 ml orange colored	6-oz FIBER flush 9 grams of fiber Miralax every 3rd day instead of fiber	**Cyprohexadine** 7.5 ml clear yellow color	Potty Time pees 3 times
8:30	Wake Up	Potty Time	Self-Help Skill		
9:00	**Lamictol** 150 mg 1 white pill in syringe with water	30-ml water flush	Breakfast		
9:30 **to** **11:30**	8 oz of water 2 of the 8 are half Monavie and half water	Potty Time	Therapy/Play		
12:30	Lunch Time				
2:00	**Reglan** 3.0 ml orange colored	**Cyprohexadine** 5 ml clear yellow color	2-oz water flush	Potty Time	
2:20	2 packets of protein and 9 grams of fiber mixed in 6 oz of water				
3:30	**Calcium** 10 ml thick white	6 oz of water 2 of the 6 are half Monavie and half water	Multivitamin crushed and dissolved in 2 oz water		
5:00	Potty Time	Dinnertime			
6:30	Potty Time	Shower Time			
7:00	Antibiotic 10 ml or 2 tsp cloudy yellow	**Clonidine** 1 pill in 10 ml of water	2-oz water flush	**Cyprohexadine** 5 ml clear yellow color	Family Time
7:30	Nighttime				
10:00	**Lamictol** 150 mg 1 white pill and 1-oz flush	**PediaSure** to make up the remainder 1100 calories needed Mix PediaSure with 6 oz of water in feeding bag Run feeding pump at 190 ml/hr			Optional Antibiotic

1 oz = 30 ml = 30 cc

Daily Journal

Date:

Behavior/demeanor:

AM # of poopies: PM # of poopies:

Extra medications given:

Daily Journal continued

Food amount and calories: _____

Breakfast: _____

_____

_____

Lunch: _____

_____

_____

Dinner: _____

_____

_____

Total calories for day: _____

Nap: yes / no

PM sleep: good / bad

Additional comments: _____

_____

_____

_____

_____

_____

Daily Journal

Date: _____

Behavior/demeanor: _____

_____

_____

_____

_____

_____

_____

_____

_____

_____

AM # of poopies: _____ PM # of poopies: _____

Extra medications given: _____

_____

_____

_____

_____

Daily Journal continued

Food amount and calories: _____

Breakfast: _____

_____

_____

Lunch: _____

_____

_____

Dinner: _____

_____

_____

Total calories for day: _____

Nap: yes / no

PM sleep: good / bad

Additional comments: _____

_____

_____

_____

_____

_____

Daily Journal

Date: _____

Behavior/demeanor: _____

_____

_____

_____

_____

_____

_____

_____

_____

_____

AM # of poopies: _____ PM # of poopies: _____

Extra medications given: _____

_____

_____

_____

_____

Daily Journal continued

Food amount and calories: _____

Breakfast: _____

_____

_____

Lunch: _____

_____

_____

Dinner: _____

_____

_____

Total calories for day: _____

Nap: yes / no _____

PM sleep: good / bad _____

Additional comments: _____

_____

_____

_____

_____

_____